THE WELFARE OF THE MIDDLE CLASS
Changing Relations in European Welfare States

Remo Siza

First published in Great Britain in 2022 by

Policy Press, an imprint of
Bristol University Press
University of Bristol
1–9 Old Park Hill
Bristol
BS2 8BB
UK
t: +44 (0)117 374 6645
e: bup-info@bristol.ac.uk

Details of international sales and distribution partners are available at
policy.bristoluniversitypress.co.uk

British Library Cataloguing in Publication Data
A catalogue record for this book is available from the British Library

ISBN 978-1-4473-5999-9 hardcover
ISBN 978-1-4473-6000-1 ePub
ISBN 978-1-4473-6001-8 ePdf

The right of Remo Siza to be identified as author of this work has been asserted by him in
accordance with the Copyright, Designs and Patents Act 1988.

Cover design: Clifford Hayes Design
Front cover image: © William Barton / iStock
Bristol University Press and Policy Press use environmentally responsible
print partners.
Printed in Great Britain by CPI Group (UK) Ltd, Croydon, CR0 4YY

Contents

Acknowledgements

In writing this book, I have benefited from the advice and feedback of many colleagues and friends. Thanks to the referees for helpful comments on the book proposal and the earlier versions of this book. Thanks to Alex Robertson, Pete Alcock and Pierpaolo Donati, who encouraged me to study poverty, the middle class and social policies from an international perspective. I am grateful to the countless English universities that I have visited over the years, offering welcoming places and relationships, helping me to reflect and write.

During its many revisions, the book has benefited from the encouragement and advice of many colleagues, members of the Social Policy Association and other international associations, and my friends at the Anglo American Academy.

A huge thanks to Laura Vickers-Rendall and the rest of the editorial team at Policy Press for their excellent support, time and kindness. I am grateful to Chris Sakellaridis and Qasir Shah. They gladly helped me with the spontaneous and unrestrained willingness of a childhood friend, although I met them by chance only a few years ago.

A special mention to my wife Angiola, my son Nicola and his partner Martina, and finally Tommaso, the newcomer to whom the book is dedicated.

Introduction: An individualised middle class

The radical activism of the middle class

Over the course of the past two decades, in all Western European nations, the middle class has lost various certainties related to work stability and income, and is exposed to an equal number of uncertainties in other spheres of life, such as family and welfare. A large part of this class feels that typical middle-class jobs are disappearing and that it has lost the economic and social conditions and welfare benefits needed to achieve one's life project through individual action and effort, thus respecting and reinforcing the social order and civic coexistence.

Empirical research clearly shows that the middle class is overrepresented among 'radical' voters; the growing social activism and the unpredictability of attitudes and behaviours are currently the main features of the middle class both in public and private spheres of life. The middle-class individual and collective radical activism is often not easily manageable and characterised by a confusing array of aspirations and resentments.

During this period, the welfare state has undergone considerable changes. The different 'worlds' of European welfare states seem progressively less capable of addressing the needs and preferences of a large portion of the middle class, especially of its lower segment. Reforms and recalibrations of the programmes and instruments that were created in recent years (stronger politics of retrenchment, politics of austerity, new forms of dualisation, conditionality) in many cases have reduced the capacity to protect the middle class from the growing risk of instability, while doing little to foster social mobility or improve social and economic conditions. The impact on the middle class, mainly in terms of financial constraints, loss of economic security and economic opportunities and the risk of exposure to short-term and occasional poverty, is high and underestimated by policymakers and most social and political actors.

The growing disparity between the living conditions of the middle class and the capacity of public and private welfare to support their living conditions is the focus of many parts of this book.

The radical activism of significant segments of the middle class is creating growing social and political instability and is increasing support for configurations of welfare that exploit and exacerbate existing economic and social divisions. Anger and resentment against institutions and some target groups are forging the moral identities of a vast stratum of middle-class people. The issue is not hyper-individualism in abstract terms but the rise

1

of a kind of individualism (anti-establishment, against all rules, anger as a powerful driver of collective action) that Western societies and contemporary institutions are no longer able to address.

Working and middle-class interest in defending the traditional welfare system is changing. Popular support for traditional redistributive policies has declined. A considerable part of the middle class adheres to anti-immigration stances and expresses dissatisfaction with mainstream parties and the main institutions. These social strata are increasing their pressure towards a new configuration of welfare that restricts access to benefits or lowers the level of benefits for immigrants, ethnic minorities and traditionally undeserving groups. Their core ideology is a combination of nativism, authoritarianism and populism (Mudde, 2007: 26).

At the same time, significant segments of the middle class take on a different kind of activism and constitute the main social basis of many social welfare movements against the discrimination and the exclusion of the low-income families and ethnic minority groups. The middle class contributes to many contemporary movements which are aimed at preventing and solving poverty and child poverty, at fighting for the social justice of refugees and migrant workers or at tackling discrimination of people with disabilities and mental health service users.

The theoretical framework underpinning the research

A large and growing body of literature has investigated the radical activism of the middle class and its changing relation to the welfare state as a linear effect of relative deprivation or as a reaction to the profound cultural changes in Western social values. The book's overall aim is to propose an alternative perspective and a broader analytical structure, taking into account the specific social context in which the dynamics of deprivation and cultural changes happen. In every social context, several causal forces exist and interfere with each other (Bhaskar, 1979; 2008; Archer, 2007). The generative power of transformation by relative deprivation is not fixed but contingent, it is conditioned by the context that can hinder or increase the generative capacity of a single causal relationship (Porpora, 2015: 235). Middle-class relative economic deprivation or cultural changes emerge in a pre-existing social context that can remove or counter these causal mechanisms (Pawson and Tilley, 1997). Therefore, we need to understand the context in which causal mechanisms such as economic deprivation and cultural backlash lead to either radical collective protest, to moderate popular reactions or to multiply the individual effort to escape to a non-desired social position.

Globalisation, technological innovations, ecological crises and intensification of individualisation have not only affected household income, work and economic life. All over the world, they are creating processes, dynamics, interdependencies, interest groups and expectations that we are no longer able to govern. Over the past two decades, a long-lasting transition is simultaneously and radically changing, to different degrees, all the contexts where people live, all the institutions, destabilising all the certainties upon which modern societies are founded.

In a complex transition (Beck, 1992; Beck and Beck-Gernsheim 2001), radical processes are transforming the basic institutions of society, from the family to structures of governance, the everyday, ordinary lives and values, and are forcing a redefinition of intimate and personal aspects of our lives, such as the family, gender roles, sexuality, personal identity, our interactions with others and our relationships with work (Giddens, 2006: 67; 1994b). The transition not only changes social structures, but also revolutionises the coordinates, categories and conceptions of change itself. Western societies are still 'modern' societies; modernity has not vanished, yet it is becoming increasingly problematic (Beck et al, 2003: 2). The new capitalism is characterised by feverish transformations in every sphere of life which are threatening particularly those qualities of character which bind human beings to one another and furnish everyone with a sense of sustainable self: respect, pursuit of long-term goals and trust (Sennett, 1998: 29).

The starting point of my book is the radicalisation of the processes of individualisation, that are to be understood as a structural characteristic of highly differentiated societies, and which institutions are unable to manage in the current competitive and globalised setting. With the term individualisation, many authors (Parsons, 1937; 1978; Elias, 1991; Giddens, 1991; 1993; Beck, 1992; Beck and Beck-Gernsheim, 1995; 2001) do not intend to merely indicate individual choice, but also a structural characteristic of a highly differentiated society. They state that individualisation means the need to develop individual life projects moving away from traditions and collective identifications such as political parties, unions or the family, and the need for self-realisation in independently pursuing not only economic interests, but also caring relationships and collective interest. The individualisation that was previously claimed by a few people is now being imposed on all people: it is a constraint and also a compulsion to lead a life of one's own but at the same time it is a desire and an opportunity that releases people from the constraints of tradition. An increasing social differentiation is accompanied by a standardisation of social expectations, of cultural references, and of the projects for the future of the majority of people. The processes of individualisation, intensified by globalisation and technological changes, have radically transformed the foundations of everyday life.

Many authors see individualisation as a danger to society and individuality itself, however, the majority believes that integration and individualisation do not stand in opposition to each other. The primary references of my analysis are the two leading theorists of individualisation: Parsons and Beck. Other authors, such as Elias, Habermas and Bauman, help us to understand the risks and opportunities that accompanied every process of radical individualisation which may result in high fragmentation and instability of social relationships, the undermining of the central institutions of contemporary society and, for many people, a desired open way of life. There are several significant differences among these authors with regards to the outcomes of this transition. We can identify three compelling perspectives:

- Starting with Parsons, many authors emphasise the integrative nature of individualisation; it is not a symptom of the crisis, but rather a consequence of a functional process of differentiation that, through a linear route, recreates the social system, heightening both the freedom and autonomy of individuals.
- Overall, for Bauman, individualisation is a divisive force, dividing instead of uniting. The individual risks becoming an isolated monad with weak and fragmented bonds. The prospect for a 're-embedding' of individualised actors is slim.
- Beck, in line with Elias, argues that individualisation is an ambivalent process and involves both the differentiation of one individual from another and the integration into society.

These different conceptualisations have significant implications for public policy, can shape policies and legitimise different organisations of welfare services and promote different relationships between state, market and the informal sector. In countries where the main social and political subjects adopt Bauman's conceptualisation, collaborative and care resources, it is likely that the informal sector may be deemed irreversibly too weak to support welfare projects. The resources of the market are deemed crucial for the design and the providing of welfare services. In other countries, the second conceptualisation outlined shapes policies and welfare support in a linear development without significative recalibrations. Finally, there are countries where social and political subjects recognise the ambivalences and opportunities of this transition and mobilise the care and social inclusion resources that every sphere of life (informal relations, welfare, market and work system) can ensure for improving living conditions.

'Disembedding' without 're-embedding' processes

Parsons (1937; 1978), Elias (2001), Beck (1992) and Beck-Gernsheim (2001) consider individualisation as a product of complex and high-level socialisation that involves both the differentiation of one individual from another and integrating those individuals into society. The process of individualisation can be understood as an ongoing social process of 'disembedding' and 're-embedding', of being dis-established and re-established. In the long-lasting transition from a simple modern society to the second modern society in which we are living, the relation between 'disembedding' and 're-embedding' does not take a linear form.

Considerable literature has grown up around the theme of the decline in contemporary societies' ability to promote social stability and to produce mechanisms of reintegration after the 'liberating' effects of radical transformations. In many cases, disembedding processes are not balanced out by re-embedding pressures, and institutions and norms do not promote any significant re-embedding strategies: extended transformations erode traditional institutions (collective organisations, traditional family and informal relations) but they do not create new ties and new stable aggregations. On the one hand, a multitude of individual and collective subjects are continuously promoting new processes of the 'disembedding' of institutions, relations and values, in endless initiatives of 'detraditionalisation' as opposed to 'embedding'. These 'disembedding' processes weaken intermediate structures, such as the family, collective belonging and associations, and are changing informal relations.

On the other hand, our societies do not find social resources, subjects, social groups or associations able to face these dynamics of 'disembedding' and are not able to build new integrative forces, institutional resources, new forms of sociality or belonging, which might help individuals to actively live in a highly individualised society. Altruistic and cooperative processes of individualisation, organisations such as mutual aid groups, parent groups and community-based forms of solidarity are not strong enough to create a new culture of human relations. In the welfare sphere, many social and political subjects wish to dismantle traditional sectors, while a smaller number of individual and collective subjects wish to promote a more inclusive welfare system and improve the ability of institutions and people to work together for a common purpose.

Several authors highlight that what is underway is not a new social order, but an ongoing interregnum, a prolonged emerging period of social entropy that does not provide templates for social action and social existence (Streeck, 2016) towards a situation in which social actors take on full autonomy in relation to the system (Touraine, 2014). Rosa (2015) stresses the phenomena of desynchronisation and social disintegration resulting from accelerated transformations of social circumstances, institutions and relationships in different segments of society to different extents. Significant desynchronisation phenomena caused by differing speeds of transformation and adaptation appear in regards to both functional systems (for example, the speed of change in education is slower than that in the economy and technology sectors) and different social groups:

> [W]hat is decisive for the understanding of contemporary societies is the fact that territories, ethnic groups, financial and ideological streams as well as forms of cultural religious, and political practice are tending to become independent from one another, such that these streams can flow in various directions – i.e. in almost arbitrary (re)combinations but also largely beyond intentional control. (Rosa, 2015: 109)

Juul (2013: 150) argues that the second modernity clearly separates itself from the first modernity in which a relatively fast re-embedding process is followed by the 'disembedding' of individuals from traditional structures in new social structures such as nation, class and core family. The contemporary transition has a significantly longer lifespan than the previous transitions.

In the following chapters, I will argue that this research helps us to understand growing social instability and the unpredictability of the attitudes and the behaviour of the majority. Many factors lead us to believe that there is a growing gap between the radicalisation of every process of 'disembedding' and our societies' ability to manage and include active individuals who are disconnected from traditional forms of collective belonging.

The old and the new 'middle mass'

In contemporary modernity, new forms of mobile life, new kinds of daily experiences and new forms of social interaction emerge (Elliot and Urry, 2010: 3–4), man and woman have no permanent bonds and flexibility has replaced solidity as the ideal condition (Bauman, 2000). The self is, for everyone, a reflexive project, a more or less continuous interrogation of the past, the present and the future (Giddens, 1991: 30).

All the European societies promote individualism, but many fail to institutionalise the kinds of individualism deemed functional for their growth. Institutionalisation mean that values and norms become embedded in a social system of interrelated role expectations and norms. Once institutionalised, expectations and norms limit the ways in which individual actors can choose and pursue their goals (Verschraegen, 2011).

In all Western European countries, a large number of middle-class and working-class individuals have limited access to economic, social and cultural resources needed to face the growing risks of a globalised society and are experiencing instability and mobile life as a risk rather than an opportunity. They feel left behind in economic and social competition and can express high levels of anger against the economic and political establishment.

In the centre of social stratification, a multitude of people with unstable collective ties and fragile social identities are emerging. This multitude is particularly marked by the social life explored by authors Bauman, Beck and Giddens: it is characterised by constant mobility, vulnerability and an inclination to constantly change relationships and identities. Their social aggregations and associative forms are fragile, transient and under constant transformation. This is a mobile aggregate of people with blurred class boundaries that drifts within society, 'liberated' by processes of individualisation and fragmented in unstable belonging, with internal divisions and a frail collective identity. To various degrees, they do not believe in the established order's legitimacy and feel they are in a shared situation of economic difficulty, lacking security, status and trust in the future.

In many ways, they are a new social stratum, which no longer has any meaningful relationship with the upper middle class and views the bottom of the social stratification with fear and worry. The differences between this social stratum and both the established middle class and multiple disadvantaged groups are increasing.

In the 1970s, Wilensky (1975: 118–119; 2002) named a similar intermediate stratum, comprised of a large part of the middle class and the upper working class, the 'middle mass'. Wilensky's middle mass is a product of first modernity. Lash (1999) highlights that in a first modernity, the process of individualisation developed only partially: it demolished traditional structures (extended family, religious groups and village community), but, at the same time, it created new structures (nuclear family, national trade unions, political parties, large hierarchical firms and associations).

The current extended social stratum encompasses many of the social groups of Wilensky's middle mass. It is a product of a second modernity. Since the 1990s, the intensification of individualisation has freed the individual from the forms of social belonging developed in the last century (Lash, 1994). In opposition to the Enlightenment rationality of progress, order and homogeneity, this contemporary modernisation has initiated a different rationality based on reflexivity, uncertainty, transience, experiment and the unknowable (Lash, 1999).

Unlike Wilensky's passive middle mass, this extended social stratum is a sort of a multitude of individuals characterised by radical activism. The new 'middle mass' has to face processes of radical individualisation which weaken traditional forms of belonging and social ties, make unstable new forms of sociality and create overlaps between new and old values and beliefs. They do not have a collective and shared project of upward mobility like the traditional middle class and the working class, but just many individual projects almost always incompatible with each other.

These segments of the middle and working classes constitute a deep new social division that is altering the structure of the social stratification. Class identification, the extent to which they identify as middle- and working-class members, is still robust but becomes blurred in collective actions and voting behaviours. Living conditions in these social groups are of a more mobile nature, as they experience frequent upward and downward swings of income. In the past, the expansion of white-collar employment provided more job opportunities to new generations and created conditions for upward mobility. Today, however, as the middle class is shrinking, and there are fewer elite occupations, the opportunity for upward mobility for those born in working- and middle-class families has been declining (Payne, 2018: 21–23).

In many respects, this separation constitutes the social structural base of a new cleavage that weakens traditional left–right divisions based in the working class (left-wing political parties) or the middle class (conservative parties). For many authors (Lipset and Rokkan, 1967; Bartolini and Mair, 1990; Kriesi, 1998; Badie et al, 2011) the notion of a cleavage includes three essential elements: a social-structural element; a sense of collective identity; and the willingness to organise durable collective actions. This term identifies social and political divisions characterised by a close connection between the positioning of individuals in the social stratification, their beliefs and normative orientations, and their behavioural patterns. This close connection contributes to the stability of cleavages over time.

In this new social cleavage, a shared set of cultural attitudes, beliefs and values grows, which are quite often against the establishment and political institutions. Over the last two decades, this social cleavage has been constituting the basis for the organisation of relevant interests and mobilising people around a sense of injustice. Confidence in institutions, civic values and trust in other people have been declining among the members of this cleavage.

Towards a 'third welfare system'

Various scholars have long noted that the evolution of the welfare state in the second part of the last century conferred disproportionate benefits to the middle classes. These included better access to social programmes and a higher quality of service in areas like healthcare, childcare and education. At the end of the 1950s, Brian Abel-Smith (1958) points out that the middle class was the major beneficiary of welfare and gained more from the welfare state than the working class. Titmuss (1958), in his seminal work on the social division of welfare, identified three systems of welfare: social/public, fiscal and occupational. All three systems favour the middle and upper classes: the higher income groups know how to make better use of the services. Instead, the poor have great difficulties in managing change, choosing between alternatives and finding their way around the complex world of welfare (Titmuss, 1958: 19).

In the last two decades, social policy responses to the economic and social decline of middle class have been weak. New forms of dualisation and the politics of retrenchment have reduced the ability of welfare to address the needs not only of households in a condition of poverty, but also those of the central classes of the social stratification. In Europe, many authors highlighted that the dualisation in terms of access to benefits, efficiency and quality of services has an impact on a large majority of the population (Emmenegger et al, 2012: 10). The protection offered by the public system is no longer sufficient and the population is increasingly divided between those who can access private protection (mainly, the established middle class) and those (a large part of the middle and working class) who are at risk of having both inadequate public services and limited access to private insurance and occupational schemes. Low-income households can only access public services with varying degrees of quality depending on geographical areas, targeted groups and sectors of intervention.

To various degrees, from Scandinavian countries to France, Germany or Italy for example, European welfare systems are heading towards a divided welfare state, that is two very different welfare states within one country. One of these welfare states, the hidden one, is emerging through government support given to certain social groups that have the economic resources and the formal right to benefit from it. This hidden welfare state grows at the expense of the universal welfare state, which has traditionally been used by everyone (Lapidus, 2019: 235–236). In the US, Hacker (2002) documents and analyses the new divided public and private social benefits system. 'Social insurance', the heart of the welfare system for the non-poor, has been constructed to protect the integrity and dignity of the people involved. Many social welfare duties are handled not by the state, but by the private sector with government support. Private social benefits have deeply influenced the politics of public social programmes.

Over the course of the past two decades, another division is emerging. An increasing body of research demonstrates that a growing number of people are being forced to turn to charitable food aid to satisfy their basic need for food. Evidence suggests that this rise in food charity has occurred in the context of increased conditionality and reduction to entitlements in social services (Lambie-Mumford, 2019; Lambie-Mumford and Silvasti, 2021) and from a delegation of responsibility of caring for those experiencing food insecurity from the state to the charitable sector (Parsell et al, 2022).

In the last two decades, following the age of dualisation discussed by Hacker and Emmenegger, the public system traditionally aimed to replace dependence on the charity sector instead is supporting the development of a strong 'third welfare system'. A significant number of public welfare sectors have been paying growing attention to race, ethnicity and beneficiary behaviour, introducing severe conditional measures and multiple discrimination in access to benefits. The increasing conditionality placed on some groups deemed less deserving and aggressive chauvinism constitute key dimensions of planned government reforms. The main social, economic and political actors believe that being more selective, increasing the degree of conditionality and lowering the level of benefits for deserving groups and immigrants are priority measures.

The 'third welfare system' is the welfare for some groups of the 'precariat', mainly ethnic minorities, asylum seekers, some people with disabilities and a growing number of ex-convicts. It is a 'poor' welfare only for the old 'underclass', that is, those who experience chronic poverty, do not have a relationship with the world of production, and are detached from common values. Still, it is also the welfare for the new 'white underclass', a land of broken families, pain and despair, and few prospects (Murray, 2013; Case and Deaton, 2020).

The result is a decrease in public welfare claimants. Only a number of them, varying from country to country, improve their social conditions, escape from welfare dependency and conditions of material deprivation and can finally access the benefits and services ensured by private providers. In contrast, a large number is detaching from welfare services and turning to the 'third poor welfare system' provided by many charities and local public institutions that distribute basic goods for day-to-day living and ensure temporary economic support. More so than the reduction of local authority funding, it's the punitive shift that has fundamentally altered certain policy areas of welfare and its relationship to certain social groups. It has increased its interaction, similarities and links with welfare programmes specifically targeted to the homeless, minority groups and social tenants. The penal system is looming over this welfare and its claimants and can be used as a threat or the final sanction for persistent irregular behaviour. The punitive shift has surely led to an increase in the prison population which has disproportionately affected low-income and minority populations (Cummins, 2021). However, the penal system is not replacing the welfare state in regulating the old and new 'underclass' expelled from public welfare: in many European countries, the 'third welfare system' is the main way to manage these undeserving groups and ensure their minimal integration.

In recent years, a large part of the middle classes has not objected to divisive configurations of welfare, as it responded to a new desired social identity founded on individual agency and self-reliance. At the same time, within the middle class new collaborative relationships, new opportunities for social dialogue and alternative ways of looking at the world are emerging. Significant segments of the middle class are promoting active social initiatives capable of strengthening civic values and trust in other people and are contributing to rebuilding a sense of collective belonging and identity.

Defining the middle class: the need for a multidimensional approach

In Western European countries, the majority of people live in middle-class households but do not experience shared conditions of economic security, status and trust in the future. The term middle class covers a broad spectrum of people with different opportunities in life, qualifications, remuneration and social identity (Crompton, 2008). The middle class consists of people who occupy social positions that provide them with material and cultural advantages (Giddens, 2006) and who, therefore, wish to defend the status quo. At the same time, the middle class consists of low-income and status-precarious people who demand deep social change; this segment constitutes the majority. In Western European countries about 50–60 per cent of the population lies in this central area of the social stratification (Pressman, 2017).

The term middle class has no commonly agreed definition and there is much instability between the different groupings that are said to make up the middle classes (Butler and Savage, 1995; Crompton, 2008). Much empirical research tries to operationalise the concept of the middle class by employing occupational and employment status based on schemes such as the European Socio-Economic Classification (ESeC) known as the Erikson-Goldthorpe-Portocarero (EGP). This scheme (Goldthorpe, 1987; Erikson and Goldthorpe, 1992; Rose and Harrison, 2007) distinguishes four basic employment positions: (1) employers; (2) the self-employed; (3) employees; and (4) those involuntarily excluded from paid employment. In this scheme, the term 'middle classes' includes: lower-grade professionals and managers (class 2); intermediate classes and lower supervisory and technicians (classes 3 and 6); small employers and self-employed non-professional occupations (class 4); self-employed occupations (class 5); lower services, sales and clerical occupations (class 7).

In the 1990s onwards, many authors discussed whether it is useful to continue to regard classes as primarily employment-based entities (Savage and Butler, 1995: 351). Much of the recent comparative research on the middle classes relies on income-based definitions because data on income is widely available and is correlated with economic security and education level (Bigot et al, 2012). Typically, being middle class is defined as having an income within a scale constructed around the median and which has typically been symmetric. This definition became the most commonly used one in empirical studies of the middle class (Pressman, 2007).

The definition of the lower cut-off point has a natural link with the poverty threshold, which is set at 60 per cent (European Union) or 50 per cent (OECD) of the national median equivalised disposable income. Lester Thurow, the first author that adopted this approach (1984), defined the middle class as including households with an income between 75 and 125 per cent of median household income. However, in contrast to the poverty threshold, which refers to a condition where income is insufficient to maintain the minimally acceptable living standard, the middle class thresholds have a high degree of arbitrariness (Ravallion, 2010).

Many authors, using a different range of median income, divide the broad category of the middle class into two groups: the lower middle class and the upper middle class (Atkinson and Brandolini, 2011; Bigot et al, 2012). Whelan et al (2017) take those between 60 per cent and 75 per cent of the median to be 'precarious' or on the 'margins' of poverty. The middle class can then be said to be those not in poverty or in the margins of poverty, between 75 per cent (lower thresholds) and 166 per cent of the median (upper thresholds). Within this they distinguish a 'lower middle class' between 75 and 125 per cent of the median and an 'upper middle class' between 125 and 166 per cent of the median. Those whose incomes are at least 167 per cent of the median are considered as the affluent class (pp 7–8). In other approaches, the middle class is defined using the distribution of households in a country by income quintile (second to fourth income quintile). The OECD (2019) adopts an income-based definition using the term 'middle-income class', rather than 'middle class'. The report defines 'middle-income class' as the population living in households with an income ranging between 75 and 200 per cent of the national median (p 19).

In many aspects, it is useful to adopt an income-based definition in international comparative analyses or a definition based on employment relationships. However, I am aware of the need to overcome approaches based on the observation of a single economic variable for many reasons. The high correlation between income, employment position and other indicators of social status has weakened in recent years. Especially among many intermediate groups the condition known as 'status inconsistency' is growing, attributable to the modest correlations between income, occupation and education (Hodge and Treiman, 1968). People understand what goes into being middle class in the abstract, but many find themselves in complicated positions that imply different class identities and incongruences among very different positions that an individual can occupy (Hout, 2008: 31–32). Differences in terms of education, social capital or professional skills usually do not create clear social outcomes in terms of upward social mobility and higher income. Status inconsistency between the positions that individuals hold in different spheres of life affects well-being and creates feelings of uncertainty and social conflicts over the definition of appropriate social identity and social rules.

Moreover, within the middle class we can distinguish social groupings that share common income conditions and employment relations which are, however, very different to other groups of the same class. There are growing differentiations between the middle class in terms of networks of relationships, levels of trust and cultural capital as symbols, tastes and preferences, which can be used as resources in social action.

In order to propose a concept of class which does not reduce it to the measurement of a single key variable, other authors have developed a multidimensional way of registering social class differentiation not exclusively based on employment or income, but on the interplay between economic, social and cultural capital (Savage et al, 2015) and have explored the cultural dimensions of class, gender and ethnicity across a range of fields (Bennett et al, 2009). Following Bourdieu's steering, Savage et al (2015) define a new model of social class which shows how measures of economic, cultural and social capital can be combined to provide a powerful way of mapping contemporary class division. The resulting structure names two middle classes: the established middle class, with high economic, social, and cultural capital and more social contacts than any other social class; and the technical middle class, with more moderate cultural capital and few social contacts but otherwise high economic and social capital. The latter competes with the established middle class to be the second most prosperous class in terms of economic capital. However, socially and culturally, it is much more restricted than the established middle class. They also draw attention to new affluent workers whose household income is moderate, and who have a small amount of savings. This group is therefore economically secure without being very well off. Its members score the second highest on their number of social contacts.

For many authors, the central concern is how people acquire the attributes that place them in one class or another. For most of them, people's economic status and rewards are mainly acquired through employment in paid jobs. Savage et al (2015) think that there are mechanisms of accumulation other than those arising from the labour market alone. Cultural and social capital allows those people with certain cultural dispositions and capacities, and who have certain kinds of social networks and informal ties, the potential to accumulate and acquire educational qualifications, information or skills. Welfare can encourage social and cultural capital formation.

Reconceptualising relationships between state, market and the informal sector

Social, cultural and economic dimensions of class and social mobility highlighted by the multidimensional approach to social stratification have important implications for the organisation of welfare services, particularly for activation and work–family reconciliation programmes. In a welfare project of upward mobility and personal growth, these programmes need to be able to recognise the importance of social and cultural resources and avoid measures that decrease their consistency.

In the book, I argue that key welfare programmes currently pay too much attention to labour market dynamics and underestimate the role of networks of relationships and the person's cultural resources (norms, values, beliefs) that can be mobilised in the process of social inclusion. Many welfare policies do not help middle-class families to maintain their living conditions; through increasing sanctions and intensification of welfare conditionality, there is a risk that low-income households and more marginalised claimants become excluded from the benefits.

In my view, it is possible to pursue an inclusive, non-discriminatory and non-divisive social policy strategy able to create the conditions for supporting an individual's autonomy and steering individual life projects towards cooperative and altruistic purposes. Underpinned by core values such as respect, dignity and trust, these policies can be oriented towards the strengthening of civic values, increasing individual autonomy and creating opportunities for families and individuals to take part in collective activities.

In this recalibration of social policies, the starting point is to reconceptualise the relationships between state, market and informal sector with the aim of recognising the plurality of resources which the individual can access in each sphere of life (informal relations, market, welfare).

Adopting this approach in Chapter 5, I outline some proposals for a change in key welfare programmes in order to create more collaborative relations between welfare institutions and both the majority of people and minority groups, including: taking into account the twofold conception of society as both system integration and social integration; promoting programmes more grounded in the communicative sphere and a relational state; implementing activation programmes founded on a plurality of social resources and on the need to support new forms of sociality and care.

In a highly individualised society, the task of welfare is no longer to insulate the individual from risk. Rather, the task is to construct opportunities to improve people's living conditions, to promote a social safety net and quality health and education institutions, in order to face the risks of an individualised existence and introduce rules, fairness and humanity into the market dynamics. Moreover, we need a new focus for welfare systems which is able to strengthen community relationships and the capacity of the family and the wider community to face hardships and conflicts.

Such a new welfare configuration does not place into question the need to increase labour market participation through activation programmes but operates with the awareness that personal relationships and social networks are resources that can be decisive in social inclusion processes. Social policy 'retains its traditional contribution to well-being'. If the real goal is the social integration of people, it is evident that the labour market cannot be the exclusive integrative resource.

We need, instead, to build new forms of social interaction and new ways of staying together compatible with the requirements of an individualised existence. Active social policy can contribute to rethinking the forms of sociality and the social ties that we can build in late modern society and can contribute to supporting the new kinds of social support and new care relationships that are emerging in many spheres of life. The task of an active welfare is to find a new balance between individual actions and collective order, between risk and security.

Structure of the book

The book reflects on the ability of many societies to reconcile the needs of economic growth with the quality of relationships, to manage economic changes and the social divisions which these continually create. To understand the rise of the radical activism of the middle class and its changing relations with welfare, it is necessary to carefully observe the drastic transformation of European societies. As we will see in more detail in the next chapters, this transformation increases the negative impact on the individual of economic deprivation and radical cultural changes.

In Chapter 1 I give a brief overview of the recent academic and political debate on the decline of the middle class. In this chapter, I argue that a large part of the research on the decline of the middle class captures neither the extent and intensity of the hardship endured, nor its impact on civil coexistence and the functioning of economic and political institutions. Moreover, I argue that we need to understand the context in which the dynamics of deprivation and cultural changes happen and which other causal relationships exist and could interfere with the causal power of these dynamics. These interactions offer a more productive understanding of the recent activism of the middle class and its shifting relations with the welfare state. They have also led to a profound change of the welfare needs of the middle class. This chapter sums up the public and academic debate on the recent activism of the middle class and on the role played by the unequal distribution of wealth and income on living standards or, alternatively, by the profound cultural changes in social values in many Western European nations.

The central focus of Chapter 2 is the radical individual and collective activism of the middle class. I argue that this radical activism is mainly created by an intensification of processes of second modernity individualisation that have freed people from traditional roles and constraints and undermined 'intermediate institutions' such as trade unions, political parties and ethnic groups. These changes are part of a complex transition from simple modern society to a second modern society. In this chapter, I put forward a broader analytical structure referring to the key concept of individualisation as developed mainly by Beck, Bauman and Parsons. Economic and technological changes are weakening a founding principle of competitive societies that want to valorise individual effort: that individuals are builders of their biographies, but should pursue their life projects in disciplined ways, respecting the rules and social institutions which they themselves contribute to through their active and dynamic participation in society. Over the last two decades this individualism is no longer able to promote integration in an active society of sizeable social groups.

The main theme covered in Chapter 3 is the rise of an extended social stratum in all countries of Western Europe akin to Harold L. Wilensky's (1975) 'middle mass'. It is a multitude of active and reflexive individuals, formed by the majority (a large part of the middle and working classes), which is separated and increasingly distanced from the upper-middle-class and low-income households. The 'new middle mass' is an extended social stratum that has weakened traditional forms of belonging and the social ties of the first modernity and overlapping new and old values and beliefs. This stratum of people feel that they are in a shared condition of economic difficulty, lacking security, status and trust in the future. They have a fluid social identity for the simultaneous flexibilisation of work, family and all social rights, and the perception of being an economically and political 'left behind' group. This stratum is fragmented in social cleavages grounded outside the division of labour in issues such as ethnic nationality. Collective and individual activism of this stratum constitutes one of the most significant critical issues of strategies aimed at countering social instability and the degrading of social life of contemporary societies.

The focus of Chapter 4 is the decline of the middle class and its changing relationship to the welfare state. Until the 1980s, many authors found that the middle class was in an advantageous position compared to less affluent social groups when it came to accessing public services. In recent years, welfare seems less and less capable of addressing the needs of a large part of the middle classes, especially the lower segment. A considerable amount of research shows the progressive middle class shift in welfare support. The decades of welfare retrenchment after the economic crisis of the 1970s were crucial to a radical change of middle-class welfare attitudes. In this chapter, I argue that over the past two to three decades, a strong social division emerges between the more dynamic segment of the middle class and the 'new middle mass' regarding three main aspects of welfare policies: cuts to social spending; social investment policies; and support for configurations of divisive welfare. The more educated segment with higher socioeconomic status tends to support social investment programmes, while a large part of the 'new middle mass' supports and defends the welfare state and requests better protection for the losers of globalisation. They believe that selective cuts to social spending and some politics of retrenchment are necessary, reasonable and fair because some recipients do not deserve welfare benefits, and migrants and asylum seekers make excessive use of welfare.

In Chapter 5, I note that the radical transformation of traditional and new social ties, the erosion of the ordinary capacity of collective welfare institutions, and rapid changes in values are signs of a metamorphosis of society that many middle mass members fail to control and address individually. For an understanding of these changes, it is necessary to more carefully observe the complex nature of the transformations affecting the welfare–market–family relationships. In many European countries, welfare institutions are unable to manage the sweeping transformation of traditional and new social ties and rapid changes in values. The transformations that are taking place in family relations, resources of support and sociality and their needs are deemed to be substantially restricted to some social groups and can be addressed with divisive and targeted configurations of welfare. In this chapter, I outline some proposals for welfare reform, suggesting a reconceptualisation of the relationships between state, market and the informal sector: a welfare grounded on the communicative sphere; a relational state; activation programmes founded on a plurality of social resources; and the need to support new forms of social interaction that are emerging.

In the Conclusion, I assert that the welfare of the middle class has been reconfigured towards progressive deregulation and privatisation of welfare policies, increasing state control over public welfare expenditure, and a stronger emphasis on the importance of individual choice and individual responsibilities. A large part of the current welfare changes is increasing the hardship and instability experienced by the middle class; these changes are not capable of managing more problematic social groups. The impact on the living conditions of these groups is high and underestimated by policymakers and the majority of social and political actors.

In the last few years, dualisation, conditionality and chauvinism constitute key dimensions of the new welfare proposed by European governments that a large part of the middle classes has not objected to, as it responded to a new desired social identity. Using Hall's concept, we can say that there has been a 'paradigm shift' in last three decades in this topic: policymakers work within a framework of ideas that specify the policy goals and the kind of instruments that can be used to attain them, but also the very nature of the problems they are meant to be addressing (Hall, 1993: 279). In my view, the limits of this welfare paradigm are evident. It is not based upon ideas or policy goals that recognise the relevance of increasing welfare capacity to address the needs of the central classes of the social stratification and minority groups. However, in policymaking, paradigm changes may be swift.

1

The radicalisation of middle-class activism: a theoretical overview

Two well-established strands of research

A considerable body of theoretical and empirical research has documented that a large part of the middle class perceives to have lost the economic and social conditions and welfare benefits needed to realise their life projects. The decrease in the disposable income of middle-class households and reduction in opportunities for upward mobility has contributed to creating a feeling of 'stabilised hardships' that seem increasingly difficult to overcome. Even in more dynamic European societies, the job polarisation between the increase in low-paying and high-paying occupations and the shrinking of middle-paying occupations is growing. This polarisation limits the opportunities for upward mobility for many workers with middle levels of education. Many of them feel they live in an uncertain situation: for a number of different reasons, they cannot change their middle-class way of life, but the awareness of the growing risks they may encounter in many choices makes day-to-day life more difficult and the final results are too often deemed unfair.

Several studies have found correlations between the economic and social insecurity of a large segment of the middle class, its resentment and profound distrust of major institutions, and its support for anti-establishment parties.

Radical activism prevails rather than passive attitudes and behaviours. In his seminal study, Lipset claimed that political radicalism in the form of Fascism and National Socialism, constituted an 'extremism of the centre', a middle-class movement representing a protest against both capitalism and socialism, and big business and big unions (Lipset, 1960). This radicalism was eroding the capacity of a political system to engender and maintain the belief that existing political institutions are the most appropriate and suitable ones for society (Lipset, 1960).

In recent years, the literature stresses that in Western Europe the support of radical right populist parties is the most characteristic expression of this radical activism. Populist radical parties on the right are widely considered the most successful new party family in the past three decades (Rathgeb and Busemeyer, 2022). The heart of this 'extremism' concerns the conflict between, on the one hand, the mythical, homogeneous and unified common people (the 'hard-working' citizens), and on the other hand, an enemy that consists of a political, economic and cultural establishment. Populism is a thin-centred ideology that considers society to be separated into two homogeneous and antagonistic groups, 'the pure people' versus 'the corrupt elite'. Politics should be an expression of the general will of the 'ordinary people' against the 'untrustworthy corrupt elite' (Mudde, 2007: 543). Both the populist left and populist right hold the elite culpable, and both see themselves as victims of an institutional bias (Clark, 2020).

Populism is an individual and collective radical activism that includes all variants of collective actors (parties, movements, sub-cultural milieus) (Minkenberg, 2016) and which influences voters' behaviours and social policy attitudes of different groups in society. National populism strongly appeals to a coalition of key groups with shared values and few intensely held concerns. They are likely to feel that other groups are receiving unfair advantages (Eatwell and Goodwin, 2018: 17–22).

In a social context marked by heightened risk and offering few opportunities for social mobility, loosely organised forms of activism are growing. These are characterised by a more confused array of aspirations, anger and worries about the future. The middle class remains a central stratum in the public discourse, no longer for the integration of society, but for the radical conflicts they feed.

The social groups that express this radical activism are faced with an intensification of individualisation processes that weaken traditional forms of belonging and render unstable new forms of sociality. They are characterised by electoral volatility and temporary phases of 'dealignment' in which these groups abandon their previous party affiliations and new phases of 'realignment' to other parties (Dalton et al, 1984; Mayhew, 2000). Many parties embraced the growing individualisation and the difficulties that individuals meet in their self-realisation projects, the social divisions between winners and losers of globalisation and a competitive welfare, as a basis for their political programmes (Betz, 1993: 421).

Studies of the social basis of support for radical activism found a sort of cultural and political alliance between segments of the working class and segments of the new middle class (Betz, 1993: 421–422; Kitschelt, 1995; Giugni and Grasso, 2019); between blue-collar workers and the old middle class such as small business owners (Ivarsflaten, 2005), or between self-employed and manual workers (Givens, 2005). However, the social basis of new radicalism cannot be reduced to one single group, such as the petite bourgeoisie or the working class. According to Berger, it should be noted that populist politics are not a politics of interest representation, but it is the politics you get when interest representation has failed (Berger, 2017: 4). In a number of cases, there has been a significant 'proletarisation' of the social basis of the support of anti-establishment parties: the number of blue-collar workers supporting these parties has increased rather dramatically (Swank and Betz, 2019). Nevertheless, despite these 'proletarisation' tendencies, these parties are attracting a significant number of white-collar voters, professionals and other self-employed segments (Betz, 2004: 13).

Another significant part of the middle class takes on a different kind of radicalism. In fact, many European movements between 1968 and 1999 became precursors for the contemporary anti-globalisation movement albeit with significant differences between the more institutional 'old' left and the more autonomous and participatory 'new' political identities (Flesher Fominaya and Cox, 2013). The slogan of the '99 per cent', whose well-being had been sacrificed to the interests of the 1 per cent, became a mainstream topic in American and many European countries' political life (Castells, 2012). The Occupy Wall Street movement with the slogan 'we are the 99 per cent' thrust the issue of inequality into the centre of the nation's political conversation (Milkman, 2017). An emerging form of collectivism and activism is characterising civil society both in spite of and because of neoliberal austerity and ongoing racism, sexism, ageism and ableism (Williams, 2021: 173).

The educated new middle class of white-collar employees and professionals employed in the state sector provide the social basis of contemporary peace, environmentalist, feminist and 'woke' movements. These groups engage in protest politics demanding a more participatory and egalitarian society (Kitschelt and Hellemans, 1990; Bagguley, 2003; Alcock, 2012). Welfare movements are a significant portion of these groups, involving mental health activists, women's health movements, disability right groups united by a concern with the fundamental demand for empowerment, representation and ensuring the quality and accountability of user-centred provision (Annetts et al, 2009: 10–12).

Theoretical and empirical research highlight that economic, social and cultural changes are altering the middle class's relationship with welfare and public services. Bourdieu (2003: 56) noted that social history teaches us that there cannot be a social policy without a social movement capable of imposing it. He was referring mainly to labour movements that 'civilised' the market, but there are also other movements with opposing political goals. Significant segments of the middle class are increasing their collective pressure towards a new configuration of welfare that exploits and exacerbates existing economic and social divisions (Taylor-Gooby, 2016; Taylor-Gooby and Leruth, 2018) such as welfare chauvinism (Greve, 2019) or configurations of welfare that increase the conditionality of benefits (Watts and Fitzpatrick, 2018) for the 'undeserving' immigrant and 'undeserving' native poor. In many countries we can observe an alliance between segments of the middle class, notably clerks and the petite bourgeoisie, and the working class in support of a radical version of welfare chauvinism (Oesch, 2008).

These divisive configurations of welfare aim to reinforce the social protection of 'native globalisation losers', increasing benefits for them.

Social investment and a neoliberal agenda lose relevance. Welfare becomes a sphere of life in which many social, economic and political subjects try to reconstruct the distinctions of the middle and the working class compared to other social groups, legitimising the differences. The educated new middle class of white-collar employees is a strong supporter of social investment development and its emphasis on future distributive effects of activation, human capital formation and early childcare education. However, the literature seeking to explain the emergence of radical right parties has mainly looked at driving forces related to sociocultural issues such as immigration, European integration and (opposition to) multiculturalism, with the welfare state playing only a negligible role (Golder, 2016; Rathgeb and Busemeyer, 2022).

This chapter sums up the public and academic debate on the recent radical activism of the middle class and on its changing welfare needs. In recent years, two well-established strands of research have contributed to an understanding of the living conditions of the middle class and the rise of its individual and collective activism (Rydgren, 2007; 2015; Gidron and Hall, 2017). The main, and well-established, strand of research stresses the effects of the unequal distribution of wealth and income. The second strand places more emphasis on the changing cultural values of a large portion of the middle class. In recent years, the breakdown theory, which focuses on the attributes of personality rather than a person's social conditions, has, once again, been applied by many authors after years in which it had lost much of its appeal. Observing the interactions between economic, cultural factors and attributes of personality, many authors advance complementary approaches rather than competing with the well-established perspectives

In the final part of the chapter, I argue that it is necessary to observe more carefully the context in which these dynamics develop and the ability of people to act and modify the existing situation. The increase of economic deprivation or more radical cultural changes does not inevitably determine a rise of protest. Structural changes are always mediated by agency. Moreover, in every social context, there are many causal relationships (fragmented social fabric, increasing unemployment, new welfare programmes, collective initiatives and so forth) that interfere with the dynamics of economic deprivation or cultural changes. Their interaction can produce different individual and collective outcomes: encouraging collaborative initiatives, hindering radical protests, or fuelling radical movements.

The economic decline of the middle class

During the last few decades, a large body of theoretical and empirical research has documented the effects of the unequal distribution of wealth and income, the loss of economic security, opportunity and upward mobility (Lind, 2004;

Pressman, 2007; Krugman, 2009), and the decline in living standards of middle-class households (Parker, 2013). The unequal distribution of wealth and income is directly correlated to the growing financial difficulties of the middle classes and inequality of opportunity and outcome (Hacker and Pierson, 2010; Stiglitz, 2016). These factors have contributed to the rise and persistence of current 'middle class radicalism'.

Many authors focus on the 'middle class squeeze', a term coined by Kus (2013), referring to the decline of middle-class income and the reliance on credit to maintain established living standards. There is extensive literature on the role that factors such as technological change, the growth in international trade, market inequalities and limited social mobility have played in creating the 'middle class squeeze' (Parker, 2013: 1–6).

The middle class is being 'squeezed', in the sense that the share of people in the middle income group has declined over time, especially among the new generations. In many Organisation for Economic Co-operation and Development (OECD) countries, middle incomes have barely grown. There are now signs that make us think that this bedrock of our democracies is not as stable as in the past (OECD, 2019). In many countries, trust in political institutions is growing among those in the upper middle class while it is declining among the lower middle class (Eurofound, 2018). The European middle classes face an increasingly expensive cost of living. This higher cost of living and less secure prospects might have eroded middle-income households' ability to save.

Four in ten middle-class households are financially vulnerable, and half struggle to make ends meet. Middle-income households seldom fall into relative poverty. However, in the past two decades the probability of middle-income households sliding into low-income territory has risen (European Commission, 2020).

There are many tendencies towards job insecurity – a high incidence of low-paid workers and a high proportion of undeclared work. Many households, especially families at the bottom quintiles of income distribution, are experiencing a significant reduction of their income. However, we are witnessing economic and social conditions of many households which are much more fluid than the collective social drift or the irreversible downward mobility commonly stressed by social and political actors and by findings of considerable research. By applying Castel's concept of the three 'zones' (2003), it can be seen that the middle class is no longer the zone of integration (people with stable work and durable social relationships) but is becoming more a zone of vulnerability with non-standard employment contracts, economic insecurity and fragile social relationships. In recent years, the zone of integration has broken up and the zone of vulnerability has expanded, leading to the growing risk that segments of the middle class may feed the third, the 'zone of disaffiliation' (absence of any participation in productive activities and relative social isolation). However, the matter is not of placing the middle class in one of these 'zones', but rather of clarifying the processes that carry them from one into the other, for example, passing from vulnerability to integration, remaining in the same zone or descending from vulnerability into social nonexistence (Castel, 2003: xvii).

Lipset (1959; 1960) stressed the relationship between the level of economic development and the presence of a democratic government: 'the more well-to-do a nation, the greater the chances that it will sustain democracy'. 'Extremism of the center' or 'extremism of the middle class' has a direct relationship with economic development. Several empirical studies have continued to find significant correlations between socioeconomic variables on the one hand and political outcomes (such as free polities and human rights) on the other (Lipset, 1994: 16).

Several studies have documented that income inequality is related to support of democracy. Much research highlights that globalisation has exacerbated the long-standing interregional inequalities to a remarkable degree in many European countries. Political extremism has been heavily concentrated in territories that have suffered long-term declines reflecting the increasing urban–rural divide (McCann, 2016: xxix–xxx). Among similar lines, other authors (Horner et al, 2018; Rodríguez-Pose, 2018) documented that persistent poverty, economic decay and a lack of opportunities are the roots of considerable discontent in declining regions. Poor development prospects have led many of these places to revolt against the status quo.

In France, existing research explores the rise of the Yellow Vest movement (*gilet jaune*) as a collective response to perceptions of growing levels of inequality (Jetten et al, 2020). The protesters have high levels of concern over downward social mobility and perceive illegitimacy in the growing gap between the 'haves' and 'have-nots' and deteriorating relations between different social groups. The Yellow Vest movement is a revolt of the forgotten lower middle class from suburbs and rural areas. Most of them are employed (many in blue-collar routine jobs, routine jobs in back offices, and in administration), but are increasingly concerned with their economic well-being and future prospects in the labour market. They feel that the economic and political system is unfair and that they cannot afford the ever-increasing cost of living. The source of the populist wave in France and Italy can be found in peripheral regions. This protest is carried out by the classes that were once the key reference point for a political and intellectual world. The economic divide between peripherals and the metropolises illustrates the separation of an elite and its popular hinterland (Guilluy, 2018).

A number of studies show that the sharp increase in political extremism and the associated drop in trust in political institutions are correlated with an economic downturn. Algan et al (2017) compared European regions that greatly suffered from the crisis with those that weathered the crisis relatively well. They find that increases in unemployment are followed by rising voting shares for anti-establishment parties (far left, far right, populist and Eurosceptic) at the subnational level. The change in unemployment – rather than its level – correlates with voting for non-mainstream parties. White working-class resentment does not simply regard identity and its opposition to multiculturalism, but it also concerns day-to-day competition with newly arrived immigrants and established minority communities for public resources, including social housing, education, social services and jobs (Beider, 2015: 57; Funke et al, 2016). Despite this, the White working class continues to be framed for their opposition to multiculturalism, instead of recognising their anger in response to deindustrialisation, the decimation of working-class jobs and their political disconnection from mainstream political organisations (Beider, 2015: 170).

The cultural changes

Inglehart and Norris (Norris, 2005; Inglehart and Norris, 2016; Norris and Inglehart, 2019) argued that diminishing job insecurity and rising inequality certainly play a role in fuelling popular resentment, but the results of empirical analyses are mixed and inconsistent. Rydgren (2015) states that electoral support for the radical right can be explained not by socioeconomic preferences but can rather be filtered by sociocultural preferences. For Bornschier and Kriesi (2015), economic marginalisation and job insecurity play no role in determining votes for the extreme right. Cultural divides rather than economic deprivation lead to support the extreme right. A voluminous literature has argued that extreme populist right parties thrive on the potential constituted by the economic and cultural processes of modernisation of the past decades. Contrary to this assumption, they show that economic marginalisation and job insecurity play no role in determining the vote for these parties. A second key finding is that cultural worldview, over and above their educational antecedents, plays the most important role in determining the vote for these parties (Bornschier and Kriesi, 2015: 27–29).

Norris and Inglehart propose a cultural backlash thesis as an alternative to the perspective on economic inequality. That is to say: many social groups, such as the middle class, resent the displacement of familiar traditional norms, and feel threatened by the spread of progressive cultural changes and values, such as multiculturalism, open borders, acceptance of gender and racial equality and so forth. People react to the profound cultural changes in Western social values. Rise of progressive and post-materialist values during the 1970s in Western societies that valued diverse forms of sexuality and gender identities, lesbian, gay, bisexual and transgender (LGBT) rights, appears to have spawned an angry and resentful counter-revolutionary backlash today (Norris and Inglehart, 2019: 32–36).

Groups may react to the profound cultural changes in several ways. One strategy could be self-censorship, the tendency to remain silent. Another could be an adaptation, as groups gradually come to accept the profound cultural shift. A third could be a retreat to social bubbles of like-minded people. According to Norris and Inglehart:

> [A]n alternative strategy is the authoritarian reflex, a defensive reaction strongest among socially conservative groups feeling threatened by the rapid processes of economic, social, and cultural change, rejecting unconventional social mores and moral norms, and finding reassurance from a collective community of like-minded people, where a transgressive strongman leader express socially incorrect views. (Norris and Inglehart, 2019: 16)

Other authors (Oesch, 2008: 359) propose that in Western European countries, the decisive variables for the electoral success of right-wing populist parties seem primarily due to the fear of welfare competition and the fear that immigration undermines a country's culture. Our age of globalisation is also a time of nationalism, of ethnic mobilisation and of the rise of xenophobic movements. In this age, many people experience a loss of identity and control over their destinies and there 'is nothing beyond the nation-state that can serve as a new anchor for collective identities and that can renew the sense of control' (Koopmans et al, 2005: 4).

Minkenberg (2000: 187) highlights that the support for the radical right comes from the stratum which is rather secure but objectively can still lose something. Populist parties received significantly greater support among the less well-off and among those with experience of unemployment, supporting the economic insecurity interpretation. In terms of occupational class, populist voting was strongest among the petite bourgeoisie, small entrepreneurs, shopkeepers, merchants, self-employed artisans and independent farmers, rather than among unskilled manual workers. However, populism received significantly less support among the welfare benefit-reliant and among those living in urban areas (Inglehart and Norris, 2016: 4). Moreover, authoritarian-populism is not concentrated among the economically marginalised such as unskilled workers, those lacking college degrees, the unemployed, those living in inner cities, and those with subjective feelings of economic insecurity and lack of social mobility (Norris and Inglehart, 2019).

Rather it is cultural values changes, combined with several social and demographic factors, which provide the most consistent and parsimonious explanation for voting support for populist parties. Their contemporary popularity in Europe is largely due to ideological appeals to traditional values which are concentrated among the older generation, men, the religious, ethnic majorities and less educated sectors of society. These groups most likely feel that they have become strangers to the predominant values in their own country, left behind by progressive tides of cultural change which they do not share (Inglehart and Norris, 2016).

> The cultural backlash theory argues that a new cleavage has emerged in both party competition and in the electorate in many Western societies. Rapid cultural changes, immigration, and economic conditions have triggered an authoritarian reflex among those that feel most threatened by these changes – emphasising the importance of maintaining collective security by enforcing conformity with traditional mores, a united front against outsiders, and loyalty to strong leaders. This orientation is reinforced by anti-establishment populist rhetoric. (Norris and Inglehart, 2019: 453)

Fukuyama (2018) argues that material self-interest is important, but human beings are motivated by other things as well, motives that better explain the disparate events of the present, which he calls the politics of resentment. In a wide variety of cases, political leaders have mobilised followers around the perception that the dignity of many groups has been affronted, disparaged or otherwise disregarded (p 7). Fukuyama states that 'demand for recognition of one's identity is a master concept that unifies much of what is going on in world politics today. Identity can be used to divide, but it can and has also been used to integrate' (p xv). The radical right in many countries redefined itself as 'patriots who seek to protect traditional national identity' (p 7). Too many groups believe themselves to have an identity that is not being given adequate recognition by other members of the same society.

The mobilisation of socially isolated people

Another research strand seeks to explain the rise of extremism and the vulnerability of democratic systems to mass movements, focusing on people who are socially isolated. This approach focuses on the attribute of personality rather than a person's social conditions. In Kornhauser's theory of mass society (2017 [1959]), people cut off from normal social networks are particularly vulnerable to the appeal of radical movements. The greatest number of people available to mass movements can be found in those sections of society that have the fewest ties to the social order (p 212). In short, people who are atomised readily become mobilised (p 33).

Mass society is a social system in which there is high availability of a population with relatively weak social ties, a large number of people interrelated only as a member of a mass and who individually pressure elite to meet their needs (Kornhauser, 2017 [1959]: 39). This mass is not directly related to one another in any form of independent forms of association, they are simply an aggregate of individuals. It is a society where both elites and non-elites lack social insulation: elites are accessible to direct intervention by non-elites, while non-elites become available for mobilisation by elites (Kornhauser, 2017 [1959]: 39). This contrasts with a healthy pluralist democracy, in which both elites and non-elites are partially insulated, where intermediate groups are strong, and normal channels of influence are robust (Buechl, 2013). From the democratic viewpoint, the threat posed by mass society is less how elites may be protected from the masses and more how non-elites may be shielded from domination by elites (Kornhauser, 2017 [1959]: 30).

The weakness or absence of intermediate groups renders elites manipulable to mass pressures, as they are poorly related to society but directly accessible and permeable to mass movements. People, in turn, lack the resources to restrain their own behaviour as well as that of others. Social atomisation engenders the strong feeling of alienation and anxiety, and therefore the disposition to engage in extreme behaviour (Kornhauser, 2017 [1959]: 32).

For Kornhauser, the most significant number of people available to mass movements can be found in those who are not integrated into any broad social groupings (Kornhauser, 2017 [1959]: 212). Extremist movements are fundamentally mass movements rather than class movements:

> Specifically, although fascism tends to recruit a disproportionate number of its members from middle class and communism attracts more of its adherents from working class, these movements cannot be understood merely as political expressions of the working class and the middle class, respectively. ... Since democracy may encourage the atomisation of society it may carry with it certain self-defeating tendencies. (Kornhauser, 2017 [1959]: 14–16)

The term mass can be applied only when we deal with people who cannot be integrated into any organisation based on common interest (Arendt, 1951: 311).

Social atomisation theory has had little empirical support within the academic literature on this topic. Arendt thought that the chief characteristic of the 'mass man' was his isolation and lack of normal social relationship (Arendt, 1951: 317). Turner and Killian (1987: 390) note that subsequent study of totalitarian movements has raised serious questions about the applicability of Kornhauser's concept of mass society. Oberschall (1973: 135) argued that people mobilised for a social movement are especially likely to be well-integrated, while socially isolated people are actually less likely to join. In the empirical research of Klandermans and Mayer (2006), extreme radical right activists appeared as 'perfectly normal people', socially integrated, connected in one way or another to mainstream groups and ideas (p 269). Eatwell states that the radical right was often strongest in communities that remained strong, such as rural areas and small towns (2005: 110).

Despite these findings, mass society theory proves 'well-nigh indestructible' (Hamilton, 2001: 12). Mass society theory has lost much of its appeal in the last decade, while some of its themes such as the relation between atomised individuals and radical activism have been re-explored. Berger (2017) argues that the economic and cultural explanations of radical activism are powerful and largely mutually complementary, but they also seem incomplete. The anger over working conditions and inequality that unions once channelled into collective action now remains bottled up in desperate, angry individuals vulnerable to the appeals of demagoguery (pp 16–17).

For Hertz (2020), loneliness is a major driver for why so many people support radical activism. Loneliness is not only about feeling bereft of love, company or intimacy or ignored or uncared for by those with whom we interact (our partners, family, friends and neighbours), it is also about feeling unsupported and uncared for by fellow citizens, our employers, our community and our government (p 7). In this 'lonely century', two sets of ties need to be strong: those which connect the state to the citizen, and those which connect citizens to each other (p 35). Being lonely is not simply feeling socially isolated or lacking communal ties; it also encompasses not being heard and understood (p 40). Commenting on Arendt's studies, Hertz states (p 38) that the dimension of loneliness such as the feeling of marginalisation and powerlessness, of being isolated, excluded and bereft of status and support are a clear and growing danger in the 21st century. There is something else populists proffer: a sense of belonging that is extremely important for those who are disproportionately isolated and lacking in social ties (p 46). At this point, the challenge becomes how welfare institutions, in particular, can contribute to rebuilding social ties and people's sense of belonging.

Combinatory attempts

Highlighting the weaknesses of cultural, economic and breakdown perspectives, many authors advance alternative frameworks, viewing these explanations of the rise of populism as complementary rather than competing. In my view, two frameworks proved to be useful for understanding the complex nature of the changes affecting the middle class: Gidron and Hall's thesis on populism as a problem of social integration and the modernisation losers thesis of Betz.

Gidron and Hall state that there is considerable literature about the sources of support for radical movements. On the one hand some scholars suggest that support for the radical right or left is rooted in income inequality and high levels of unemployment. On the other, some scholars argue that shifting cultural frameworks have inspired a counter-reaction from people attached to more traditional attitudes (2019). Social scientists see economic and cultural accounts as mutually exclusive explanations of a phenomenon. The objective of Gidron and Hall is to advance a framework that can bring together these two explanations for populism.

Gidron and Hall in their research (2017, 2019) are focusing on the extent to which individuals are integrated into society. They argue that rising support for radical parties can be understood as a problem of social integration. It can be defined as a multidimensional phenomenon based on the level of social contact people have with others, the degree to which they see themselves as part of a shared normative order, and the extent to which they feel respected or recognised by others. The results suggest that increased support for populism is to some extent a reflection of failures of social integration (Gidron and Hall, 2019). Much of the discontent is rooted in feelings of social marginalisation of the people that have been pushed to the fringes of their national community and deprived of the roles and respect normally accorded to full members of it (2017).

The economic developments that have depressed the income or job security of some segments of the population have set in motion cultural developments that multiply their initial effects. Feelings of social marginalisation can follow either from the loss of a valued economic position or from the perception that the cultural elite no longer hold in high value their views (Gidron and Hall, 2017: 78).

Other studies highlight a positive relationship between 'nostalgic deprivation' and support for the radical right. People who see themselves as economically underprivileged and left behind by recent developments tend to feel culturally distant from the dominant groups in society. Elchardus and Spruyt's (2016) research findings show that support for populism is not directly influenced by a weak or uncertain economic position or by dissatisfaction with personal life or feelings of anomie. It appears foremost as a consequence of a very negative view of the evolution of society – declinism – and of the feeling of belonging to a group of people that is unfairly treated by society. Many people feel that their society is in decline, unable to live up to the new challenges posed by growing internal diversity and globalisation. They feel that the patterns of sociability, welfare provisions, economic regulations and the democratic, political capacity that supported the good life are being eroded and undermined. This decline is blamed on establishment politicians or, rather, on the fact that no convincing solution to these problems is offered by the political establishment (pp 126–127). In many cases, the boundaries between 'us' and 'them' coincide with real, geographic boundaries: decision-makers tend to favour cities, while ignoring rural people. Cramer's qualitative study (2016: 12) found that in rural areas politics of resentment had three defining elements: (1) a belief that rural areas are ignored by decision-makers; (2) a perception that rural areas do not get their fair share of resources; and (3) a sense that rural folks have fundamentally distinct values and lifestyles, which are misunderstood and disrespected by city folks. Gest (2016: 15) suggests that these communities are critical of the direction society is heading and share a narrative of 'economic obsolescence and social relegation' with a sense of nostalgic deprivation.

In explanation of the rise of the radical right or left movements, Betz combines the social breakdown theory and the relative deprivation theory (Rydgren, 2007). He believes that the two approaches are not alternative. Betz (2004) argues that the losers of economic modernisation are mainly the lower strata of society: unskilled workers or the unemployed and those immediately threatened by unemployment or social decline. People who are losers in a process of differentiation of life chances and risk falling into a new underclass and becoming superfluous and useless for society (Betz, 1994: 32). Minkenberg (2000: 187) believed that modernisation losers should be defined more broadly to include 'the second-to-last fifth' stratum of society. They are the most likely to see significant declines to their life chances, giving rise to anxiety and resentment, which, in turn, makes them particularly receptive to the radical right's resentment-based appeal. For many of them, what is at stake is the future of Western European identity and basic values (Betz, 2004: 9). Only those who are able to cope with the 'acceleration of economic, social, and cultural modernisation' can be expected to be among the winners in post-industrial societies.

For Betz (1994) populism is an attitude of people who face disorienting changes and are placed in a vulnerable economic position. 'Established subcultures, milieus, and institutions, which traditionally provided and sustained collective identities, are getting eroded and/or are being destroyed and are giving way to a flux of contextualised identities' (Betz, 1994: 29).

During the 1990s, many right-wing populist parties in Western Europe turned into a new type of working-class party. Working-class disenchantment and profound distrust of major social and political institutions can be interpreted as the result of the relative economic deprivation of these groups and an increasing social and cultural fragmentation.

Betz highlights that blue-collar workers are hardly the only significant social group supporting these parties in the last two decades. The radical right has also attracted a significant number of white-collar voters, professionals and other self-employed segments – groups that are generally more likely to profit than to suffer from structural change (Betz, 2004). However, in his analysis, what is not yet understood is the active role of the middle class. Who are the losers of economic transformations? For Betz (1993: 420), the losers were mainly the lower strata of society groups with relatively low amounts of cultural capital (Betz, 1994: 29–30); they are the marginalised sector of unskilled and semi-skilled workers, young people without complete formal education and training, and the growing mass of the long-term unemployed (Betz, 1993: 420).

The infinite causal relationships

Over the last decade, as we have seen, there has been a proliferation of research addressing the relationship between the rise of radical activism and the cultural changes or the economic deterioration of the middle class. This research has produced contrasting evidence for both economic and cultural causes and generated an intense academic and public debate. Still, many findings are only partially confirmed by other qualitative and quantitative research and sometimes are distorted by flawed assumptions and embrace misleading claims. A considerable part of research on radical activism is underpinned by political aims and does not possess a solid framework that brings together a description of the observed phenomenon and the subsequent generalisation of the research findings.

Much research has yielded significant results, but evidence on the rise of radical activism as a result of the economic deterioration of one segment or single groups, such as the petite bourgeoisie or the working class, or due to an increased level of immigration, is inconclusive (Gidron and Hall, 2017; Eatwell and Goodwin, 2018). At the same time, emphasising the role of changing cultural values, authors such as Inglehart and Norris (2016; 2019) argue that diminishing job security and rising inequality certainly have a role in fuelling popular resentment, but the empirical results are mixed and inconsistent.

Literature has emerged that offers contradictory findings. In many European countries, popular reactions to the economic decline of many groups were surprisingly muted and moderate. Voters did punish incumbent political forces regardless of whether they were of the left or right (Bermeo and Bartels, 2014: 2–4). Case and Deaton (2020) argue that it is impossible to explain despair only through a single dynamic. They believe that the decline of family, community and religion is much more important in terms of despair. These declines may not have happened without the decline in wages and job quality that made traditional working- and middle-class life possible. But it was the destruction of a way of life that is seen as central, not the decrease in material well-being; wages work through the influence of these factors, not directly (Case and Deaton, 2020: 183). The explanations that combine different approaches fail to consider several key aspects of the social context in which the dynamics of deprivation and cultural changes happen.

In my view, much research grasps single deprivations or conflicts appearing within the process of the decline of the middle class, missing the bigger picture and, thus, failing to highlight the vast and far-reaching nature of the changes and the complex transition that European societies are experiencing.

Economic and cultural changes constitute constraints and opportunities for human action but, in any case, do not determine mechanically individual and collective actions.

Events are not produced by single causes but by a complex interaction of the causal powers of the entities involved (Bhaskar, 1979; 2008). In every social context, several causal relationships exist and interfere with each other with changing and irregular development (Porpora, 2015: 235), producing different outcomes from time to time, hindering or increasing the generative capacity of a single causal relationship.

By social context, they do not refer simply to the spatial or geographical or institutional location: it is the pre-existing set of social rules, norms, values and interrelationships gathered in a place which sets limits on the efficacy of causal mechanism or which turns (or fails to turn) causal potential into a causal outcome (Pawson and Tilley, 1997: 70).

In a highly individualised context, new risks and constraints emerge, as well as widely shared expectations and growing individual responsibilities. At the same time, the relational, economic and cultural resources that create security and help individuals cope with new challenges are less and less effective.

The neglected agents' social actions

Economic deprivation, cultural changes, and the political and economic decline of the middle class do not create resentment, anger and the middle class's radical activism in a linear causal relationship. As many sociologists state, structures' causality is mediated by agency, which refers to an individual's capacity to choose actively and independently, and the causal power of their initiatives. In many cases, severe economic deprivations or radical cultural changes produce outcomes contrary to expectations, thus limiting our ability to estimate causal effects. Sociologists as Bourdieu, Berger and Luckmann, and Habermas have highlighted the continuous dialectic between structure and agency. Giddens (1984: 25) argues that the social structure is the medium but also the outcome of agents' actions; it enables and constrains the agents' social actions; structures structure action, but action reproduces and modifies structure. Bourdieu (1977) critically analysed a view of social life that studied social entities without placing them in the context of the relations that produced and sustain them. Bhaskar writes (1979: 48) that agents always reproduce or transform pre-existing social structures via their intentional activities. The new structures formed in this process function, in turn, as a condition for agents' future actions. For Archer, reflexivity is the core aspect of the agency. Reflexivity mediates the role that the objective structural or cultural power plays in influencing social action and is thus indispensable in explaining social outcomes (Archer, 2007: 4–5; Donati, 2021).

In this perspective, we observe the economic and cultural changes both in structural terms, such as the severity of deprivations or radicality of cultural transformations and in relation to agents' social actions. Recognising the agency of social actors, the landscape and the nature of the middle-class changes become more articulated and less linear. The reflexivity of actors in social interaction mediates the effects of economic and cultural dynamics, as well as elaborating action projects and ways of living that produce positive or negative outcomes and reproduce or alter their initial social positions. The different means of enacting reflexivity are closely linked to the ease or difficulty with which an individual manages to arrange household life and working requirements in a life project. Social class does not standardise these different reflexivity modes and does not offer coherent cultural values.

For example, Archer (2003) identified four reflexive modes that individuals can apply to address economic and cultural changes. She defines a more widespread mode of reflexivity in a highly individualised society as an 'autonomous reflexive individualism', focused mainly on the outcome. It is the individualism of those who, to solve their problems, will rely mainly on their own personal resources and will find it hard to establish a lasting network of friends. They tend to leave their familiar environment, stand back, and have life projects focused on working activities. Their lives are more prone to oscillate between precariousness and financial stability conditions. However, their strategic plans are developed in an open-style system, inevitably exposed to unexpected and unforeseeable contingencies. The 'autonomous reflexive' individual seems to represent the coping strategies most frequently implemented in these years by a large part of the middle class.

The second mode is defined as 'reflexive communicative individualism'. This mode of reflexivity characterised middle- and working-class segments satisfied with what they have achieved, featuring life paths that favour social integration in their specific environment and integration devoid of rifts or sudden changes. To face financial difficulties, these people tend to mobilise family support networks and make decisions seconded by those close to them in constant continuity with their immediate environment. In the case of tension between their family life and working life, they will tend to privilege the former, thus resulting in a voluntary cutting back of social relations in their working environment and overlooking job openings involving relocation.

The third 'meta-reflexive' mode describes segments of the middle and working classes that are in search of an ideal, but equally of an appropriate setting in which to express and establish the latter. Such individuals have abandoned their original background and are no longer able to benefit from traditional community support. They are characterised by constant biographic mobility that translates into a straight line dotted with varying steps upwards, sidewards and downwards. It is hard to adapt the projects they take on to their environment. There is always something wrong with them, and the individuals are forced to implement coping strategies to live in an environment they deem unsatisfactory. They tend not to be in stable employment and the family networks are subject to frequent change. Meta-reflexives are in some ways more exposed to forays into poverty than the types mentioned previously due to the difficulties they encounter both in their working environment and in the context of personal relationships. Meta-reflexive individuals constitute a growing portion of the middle class that lives with a profound sense of dissatisfaction, continually criticising their lot but failing to establish collaborative relationships and follow a project in the long term.

Archer identifies a further ideal type, defined as 'vulnerable fractured reflexive', to identify individuals whose powers of reflexivity have been suspended. Previously they possessed the power to hold an internal conversation about self and society, which allowed them some control over their relationships. Subsequent contingencies had rendered these personal powers inoperative. Now, they cannot use their subjectivity to modify their external environment; they leave their lives open to the ups and downs, and they are unable to take any action to change their condition. They are households and individuals lacking a project to believe in. They are disoriented, at the mercy of events, incapable of exercising any active control over their lives.

Many authors identify other modes of reflexivity, regarding their ability to achieve the minimisation of insecurity (Giddens, 1994) and highlighting a clear differentiation between the new middle class (reflexivity winners) and underclass (reflexivity losers) (Lash, 1994).

The spread of some modes of reflexivity creates conflicts with every process of standardisation and social control. They accompany the radical activism of many social groups at the bottom and in the middle of the social stratification.

In the following chapter, I explore research on the transition towards the second modernity and intensification of individualisation and argue that they do not replace the two well-established strands of research on economic and cultural dimensions of this decline. The research on the contemporary transition is not an alternative to the research on economic decline in the middle class and they do not compete with one other. However, the former can highlight the landscape and the social context of the decline in which the agents' social actions interact with the pre-existing set of social rules, norms and values. Hence, my approach is designed to shed more light on how economic and cultural factors fuel radical activism and support radical parties in a specific context, and can create constraints or opportunities in an individual's capacity to choose actively and independently.

Conclusion

This chapter gives an overview of the academic debate on the rise of a radical activism of the middle class. In my view, analytical tools such as relative economic deprivation, cultural changes and rising inequality help us only partially to interpret the complex middle-class transformations and their uncertain relations with welfare. The radical activism of the middle class cannot be explained simply as the effect of relative deprivation or as a reaction to the profound cultural changes in Western social values.

Such research fails to recognise both the critical role played by the context in which the economic and cultural dynamics develop and, specifically, the agency of social actors that mediates the effects of economic and cultural dynamics. These dynamics constitute constraints and opportunities for human action but, in any case, do not determine mechanically individual and collective actions. All causal relations wrestle with prevailing contextual conditions. The contextual conditioning of causal mechanisms turns (or fails to turns) causal potential into a causal outcome (Pawson and Tilley, 1997). In many cases, relative deprivation and cultural backlash are 'triggering events' that can have enormous impacts on the unstable and individualised existences of some social groups, marking a critical turning point.

This body of research does not grasp the vast and radical nature of the changes. In the next chapter, I highlight that economic and cultural dynamics have a considerable impact on social life because they develop within a landscape characterised by radical and long-lasting transition processes that shape every effect. Beck pointed out that we live in a world that is not changing, it is metamorphosing. Change implies that some things remain the same. Metamorphosis implies a much more radical transformation, in which the old certainties of modern society are falling away, and something quite new is emerging (Beck, 2016: 3–7). While crises, transformation and radical social change have always been part of modernity, the transition to a reflexive second modernity not only changes social structures but revolutionises the very coordinates, categories and conceptions of change itself (Beck and Lau, 2005: 2).

2

A long-lasting transition

Introduction

In this chapter, I argue that a large part of the research focused on the role played by relative economic deprivation and cultural backlash on the radical activism of the middle class does not capture the nature of the changes that the middle class are experiencing. Much research highlights that radical activism is a consequence of the feeling of belonging to a group of people that is unfairly treated by society or of a very negative view of the evolution of society in a sort of nostalgic deprivation (declinism and 'welfare nostalgia'). Others document that there are interacting effects between the economic, social and cultural factors: some economic factors set in motion other mechanisms (cultural, related to social integration), multiplying their initial effects and changing the living condition of the majority. The relevance of economic and cultural factors is undeniable, but these studies fail to underline that all the spheres of life which compose European societies have profoundly changed, proliferating interactions and impacts to an infinite degree.

Such research partially helps us to understand the impacts of the transition towards a second modern society. We are experiencing a long-lasting transition characterised by an intensification and radicalisation of individualisation processes involving the relation of the individual to society. This transition towards a second modern society has simultaneously contributed to produce a progressive erosion of the integrative capacity of the three pillars of the system and social integration of contemporary societies: family and informal relations, work and welfare.

In this context, new causal relations emerge that interact and conjuncturally determine social groups' complex and non-linear transformations. An event is not explicable in terms of a single causal factor or constant set of factors (Bhaskar and Lawson, 1998; Bhaskar, 2008). For example, deprivation and cultural changes produce quite different effects on different subjects in different situations. There is only a tendency of a mechanism to produce a specific event but it is not repeatable in a general way; there is no constant conjunction of events. In open systems, unlike the artificial closure characteristic of the experimental situation, mechanisms combine to produce actual event conjuncturally, that is to say, in concert with other mechanisms (Steinmetz, 1998: 177). Context plays a mediating role, and its analysis helps us to highlight the power of causal relationships of economic deprivation or radical cultural changes and the conditions required for counteracting these dynamics.

The central focus of the chapter is the crisis of the kind of individualism of people who compete in relatively ordered ways and abide by the rules and institutions that they contribute to creating through their own personal commitment and autonomy.

Since the 1980s, in Western Europe, the processes of individualisation are eroding the ordinary capacity of collective institutions to manage and include a multitude of active individuals disconnected from traditional forms of collective belonging. There is clearly a problem of erosion of the major institutions and fragmentation of day-to-day life. A long-lasting transition from a simple modern society to the second modern society is eroding the resources to produce forms of integration both in the sphere of informal relations and the institutions. All European countries encounter growing difficulties in finding and recognising forms of reintegration and to deal with new fluid and transient relationships and forms of sociability based on individualism.

In my opinion, referring to these processes could be a useful starting point to reach a comprehensive understanding of the complex middle-class transformations and their uncertain relations with welfare.

The primary references of my analysis are the two leading theorists of individualisation: Parsons and Beck. Other authors, such as Giddens, Bauman, Habermas and Elias, help me understand current dynamics and emerging trends. There are several significant differences among these authors with regard to the outcomes of this transition. Some represent an inevitably atomised future society, others a society that evolves linearly towards reassuring new modernity; still others point to a society that needs to mobilise all the resources of systemic and social integration at its disposal and invent new forms of sociality to face the ambivalences of the radical transformation.

In the current highly individualised setting, relative economic deprivation is a social matter, involving several middle-class segments, yet is experienced mostly individually by seeking biographical solutions to systemic contradictions. Economic deprivation and cultural changes are perceived and dealt with by individuals with weaker social networks, who are more concerned about their future and institutions, who struggle to manage individually old and new risks in the dissolution of intermediate institutions and stable collective belongings.

The 'institutionalised individualism': the core value of Western societies

The processes of individualisation with their emphasis on individual agency and self-reliance have undoubtedly contributed to the fragmentation of identities and group homogeneity and weakened collaborative relationships. However, according to most sociological theories, integration and individualisation do not always have to be in opposition to one other. Authors such as Durkheim (1893), Simmel (1971), Parsons (1937; 1978) and Elias (1991) have clearly highlighted the complex consequences of the processes of individualisation.

For Talcott Parsons, in particular, rising individualisation is not at all a symptom of crisis or an ambivalent process, but rather a linear reproduction of social systems, a consequence of a functional process of differentiation which heightens both the freedom and autonomy of individuals and, simultaneously, the mutual dependency of individuals in general (Sørensen and Christiansen, 2013: 57).

By deliberate contrast with the utilitarian version of individualism, for Parsons, individuals are builders of their biographies. Still, they pursue their life projects in disciplined ways, abiding by the rules and social institutions to which they themselves contribute through their active and dynamic participation in society. Parsons called this kind of individualism 'institutionalised individualism', an individualism oriented by norms and values which provides the foundations and the functioning of the central institutions of society, emphasising a culturally regulated character of individualism. This has not been primarily an anarchic individualism or a generalisation of *homo oeconomicus*, but a regulated individualism, the achievement of the individual ideally being a contribution to the building of the 'holy' community.

Societies achieve social integration in proportion to the degree of institutionalisation of individualism:

> What has marked American sociology is its preoccupation with the individual above all else, thus its extraordinary concern with the motives of individuals ('action' in sociological terms) and their mutual relations ('interaction'). Even when the focus of American sociology has shifted to institutions, its concern has been to understand how these collective forces provide either a supportive arena for the realisation of individual interactions or block their realisation. (Alexander, 1983: i–ii)

Thus, individualism is congruent with a prominent development of the pervasive presence of many varieties of association and community activities (Parsons, 1978: 202–203). 'Individual freedom' is embedded within a complex network of institutions and social relations. People that glorify their total autonomy and their individualised life have at the same time the desire to lose their autonomy in love relationships (Parsons, 1978: 313–314).

The evaluation of individuals is held in common by members of a society and is enforced by a network of norms. Institutionalised individualism has become constitutive of the structure of society (Parsons, 2017: 146). The value orientation is activistic in the sense that what is valued is not passive adjustment, but increasing the sphere of freedom of action within one's particular environments and ultimately control over the environment in general.

The process of institutionalisation is not an external imposition of values against the motivations of individuals, but a stabilisation of one and the other. Institutionalisation aims to coincide the normative order of things (what the actors should do) with the motivation of the actors (what the actors want to do) and with the distribution of resources and constraints (Sciortino, 2016: 6). It is a process which aims to reconcile order and personal autonomy, to ensure order not as an impediment to an individual's growth, but to favour it.

The key point is not the direct utilitarian conception of the rational pursuit of self-interest, but a much broader conception of the self-fulfilment of the individual in a social setting in which the aspect of solidarity figures at least as prominently as does that of self-interest in the utilitarian sense.

Restrictions on individual freedom constitute a danger. The sacrifice of individualism intended as a solution to the problems of industrial society is not indicated and is not necessary (Parsons, 1978: 321–322). The guiding principle of American society is instrumental activism.

> The society, then, has a dual meaning, from this moral point of view. On the one hand, it is perhaps the primary field in which valued achievement is possible for the individual. In so far as it facilitates such achievements, the society is a good one. On the other hand, the building of the good society ... is the primary goal of valued action. ... To the individual, therefore, the most important goal to which he can orient himself is a contribution to the good society. (Parsons, 1962: 101–102)

The expression 'institutionalised individualism' sums up and reconciles the two aspects of Parson's theorisation: one emphasising the objectivity of the social order, the other the activity of individuals. The individual moves within an action space, wherein they find both support for their action and impediments to it, both resources and constraints. Institutionalised individualism is simply this: an actor who chooses among limited resources according to the various modalities of his coexistence with others (Bourricaud, 1981: 14–15). Society sets out the rules of the game, but it leaves to each actor the task of playing his proper role. It imposes on him nothing in detail, the only obligation which it lays on the individual is to be autonomous (Bourricaud, 1981: 250).

The individualism of the middle class

In many respects, the middle class historically personified the part of society which intended to actualise the kind of 'institutionalised individualism' proposed by authors such as Parsons, with the calculated aspiration of climbing the social ladder and improving their living conditions through education and hard work (Bellah et al, 1996: 142–165). Education and work systems provided the middle class with equal opportunity and possibilities for social mobility. The middle class, one without ascriptive privileges, had a central position within this social system. Its culture was founded on basic principles of the first modernity: a normal nuclear family; regular work; moderation – a prudent lifestyle; an individualisation limited by traditional bonds and ties, and by intermediate institutions and collective patterns of life; a sexual division of labour; a protective system of welfare; and a faith in science. Likewise, the White working class expressed the importance and value of hard work and how this brought in an income that enabled an individual to become independent. Paid work and the benefits to the individual, family and community that flowed were the glue which held together different people with varying incomes and levels of education (Beider, 2015; Beider and Chatal, 2020: 115). For the majority of these classes, 'institutionalised individualism' was a dream, the dream of a world in which it was enough to educate oneself and work hard to realise one's projects with the certainty that institutions would recognise the seriousness and commitment showed.

For many years, the middle class experienced an unprecedented material improvement in prosperity. In the post-war Dutch society, the middle class improved their position through strategic investments in education, homeownership and savings. Long-term planning was possible because of various institutional certainties: the security of work and a permanent job and the certainty that investments in education are worthwhile. There was a system of social welfare arrangements to reduce the risks of unemployment, the incapacity for work and illness (Siegmann, 2019). In contemporary Germany, virtually every person and every political faction believe a sound and stable middle class is the pillar of social stability, the origin of innovation and necessary for social justice (Arndt, 2019: 35).

The middle class expressed a form of individualism that was not an anarchic individualism of impatience at all social restraints, but an 'institutionalised individualism' (Parsons, 1978: 203) that was widely functional to the improvement of society, that made possible its integration and provided the foundation of social order. This was an 'internalised individualism' promoted seamlessly by institutions, a dynamic labour market, generalised cultural values and networks of social relations. Parsons outlined how these processes of internalisation are essential in achieving order in any society.

Western societies were believed capable of promoting 'individual freedom' and, similarly, shared values, role expectations and norms which constituted the conditions to ensure this functional kind of individualism as well as coordinating the actions of a plurality of independent actors (Howard, 2007; Verschraegen, 2011: 175). The most important institutions (for example, work, school, family) are specifically and explicitly oriented towards this kind of individualism, and values and norms become embedded in the social system. Instead of traditional perspectives on individuality, in which it is regarded as the simple absence of external structures, the shift towards the individual was being driven by collective processes that involve new forms of socialisation, regulation and resource allocation, all of which promote certain forms of individuality (Howard, 2007).

The middle class is a social stratum that has experienced decades of stability of income and family and informal relations, and the opportunity to afford decent housing, cars, appliances and to send its children to above-average schools and universities. The contemporary transformations involve a large part of values, the system of work, the style of life on which the middle class has found its social identity and its strategies of distinction.

The first signs of internal crisis

In the years in which Parsons hoped for an 'institutionalised and internalised individualism' (in the 1960s and 1970s), growing poverty and inequality were delegitimising the social order and any strategy to institutionalise kinds of individual autonomy, expectations and norms. Youth movements complained about the ambiguities and contradictions of advanced industrial societies, for example, the myth of the West and Europe as frontiers of freedom and democracy. The civil rights and anti-war movements, and protests against long-held values and traditional norms of behaviour, were rooted in middle-class White youth and racial and ethnic minorities.

From the 1960s onwards, a considerable amount of literature has investigated the difficult balance between individual freedom and integrative processes: many societies emphasise order, others the absolute autonomy of individuals. Key members of German critical social theory such as Adorno and Horkheimer condemned the corrosion of established liberties and a totalising form of integration of individuals in society. Advanced industrial societies were considered stable and without opposition, culturally compact, with looming 'institutionalised and internalised individualism' – an inevitable evolution towards one-dimensional thinking and a totalitarian kind of integration that exercised profound and pervasive control which threatened individuality (Marcuse, 1964). Following workers' and radical students' movements, Marcuse argued that the 'people', previously the ferment of social change, have 'moved up' to become the ferment of social cohesion: a comfortable, smooth, reasonable, democratic unfreedom prevailed in these societies, a token of technical progress (Marcuse, 1964: 1).

In reality, the possibilities of building the preconditions that promote the kind of individualism hoped for by authors such as Parsons were not very achievable. Parsons has always recognised the high improbability that the 'institutionalised individualism' may be an orientation shared by all social groups and institutions, but has tried to identify the cultural and social conditions favouring these integration processes and possible sources of tension (Sciortino, 2016: 6). However, he placed more importance on the issue of social order over individual autonomy even though he believed it could be achieved without authoritarian regulation.

For other authors, the internal contradictions of capitalism were accelerating the long-term trend towards an opposite direction. Rather than a totalitarian kind of integration, what begins to emerge in those years is a situation that Touraine calls 'post-social' in which social actors take on full autonomy in relation to the system. The breakdown of society reaches its extreme forms when the connection between the system and the actors has broken, when the meaning of a norm for the system no longer coincides with its meaning for the actors (Touraine, 1969; 1974; 1992).

Boltanski and Chiapello (2007: 487–488) argue that capitalism is the site of permanent tension between the stimulation of desire for individual accumulation and its limitation by institutional order. This compromise can be weakened either because it loses its stimulating dimension or because it is insufficiently orientated towards the common good. Strengthening any one of its components retroacts on the others.

In many contemporary societies, in my view, this unstable compromise is close to hitting a breaking point and calls for a new relationship between the two dynamics. Over the last two decades, many societies have been less and less able to make the initiative of more significant social groups functional for the 'betterment of society'. Unlike what many European governments think, many societies fail to institutionalise kinds of individualism functional to their growth: institutions are very weak and tend to organise themselves according to their own growth logic and do not respond to the functional needs of society. Moreover, individual and collective activism is often too radical. The issue has become not to regulate the marginal urban populations but to promote integration in an active society of the vast majority of people and create preconditions for citizens' autonomy and social order.

It is increasingly difficult for many societies to promote shared values and norms, and individual autonomy. In the last two decades, several kinds of individualism have been institutionalised and embedded in the social system: initially, the individualism of the neoliberal project, later the anti-establishment individualism that emerged from uncoordinated processes, from the interactions between conflictual projects of political institutions, parties, markets and active cleavages.

Institutional strategies aimed at orienting individuals towards the collective interests are increasingly less effective and weaker compared to the dimension of the transformations already in place. The 'institutionalised individualism' fails at being a meaningful and shared reference for the initiatives of the vast majority of people. Their radical activism is overwhelming the integrative activity of the good institutions. A large part of the middle and working class is distrustful of every stable integration project. In this way, processes of 'disembedding' prevail over fragile 're-embedding' ones.

In order to explain the erosion of the main institution of modernity, Beck introduces a distinction between basic principles of modernity (such as freedom, equality and rationality) and its basic institutional solutions, two being the nation-state and the nuclear family. Contemporary societies are characterised by the transformation of the basic institutions of industrial society, while simultaneously preserving the basic principles of modernity. There has been no clear break with the basic principles, but rather a transformation of the institutional order of the first modernity that increasingly displays seemingly irreversible weaknesses in delivering social functions and individual utilities that used to be taken for granted (Beck and Lau, 2005: 525–526). Across the world, a large part of the institutional order – nation-states, political parties, trade unions, democracies, market economies, industrial enterprises, welfare systems, educational and occupational systems, families and gender roles among others – has become ineffective or dysfunctional for both society and individuals (Beck and Grande, 2010: 415).

Work as an uncertain foundation of an individualised existence

In Western Europe, the last two decades have led to a significant decrease in the numbers of the most privileged categories of workers – those with the most protection – and an increase in job insecurity, incidence of low pay, and the proportion of non-standard employment and the low transition rate from this segment of the labour market to standard contracts. Recurrent economic crises have weighed on those groups which occupy the lower section of the labour market. In particular, those who work in small enterprises; who have irregular work and do not benefit from adequate welfare benefits; individuals with weak and fragmented bonds and high dependency on the labour market. A globalised labor market magnifies all the ambivalence and social risks of the processes of individualisation and dissolves securities and life projects without finding a reasonable balance between risk and security for a large part of population.

Sennett (1998: 122) highlights that the emphasis on flexibility changes the very meaning of work as a basic sphere of life and the foundation of middle- and working-class integration. The short-term, flexible time of the new capitalism seems to preclude making a sustained narrative out of one's labour, and subsequently, a career. Yet to fail to wrest some sense of continuity and purpose out of these conditions would be literally to fail ourselves. Working life in the new economy is constantly being built and rebuilt with repeated break-ups and fresh starts, thus this obstructs one's work or career as the constituting base for one's identity (Sennett, 1998). Working life is creating a class of flexible individuals with increasingly short-term expectations.

Flexibility gives people more freedom to shape their lives. In fact, the new order substitutes new controls rather than simply abolishing the rules of the past – but these new controls are also hard to understand. Organisations that celebrate independence and autonomy, far from inspiring their employees, can arouse that sense of vulnerability (Sennett, 2006: 142). Workers are asked to behave nimbly, be open to change at short notice, take risks continually, and become ever less dependent on regulations and formal procedures. In such a system, individuals' ability to develop real commitment is undermined; something which in Sennett's words leads to a state where the 'character corrodes' (1998: 147), with a subsequent decrease in trust in other people. Many conditions impel people to look for some other social relations of attachment and depth:

> All the emotional conditions we have explored in the workplace animate that desire: the uncertainties of flexibility; the absence of deeply rooted trust and commitment; the superficiality of teamwork; most of all, the spectre of failing to make something of oneself in the world, to 'get a life' through one's work. (Sennett, 1998: 138)

Radical processes of individualisation are changing the sphere of informal relations and the institutional order and perhaps, with the same intensity, are weakening the inclusive nature of work. A large number of studies recognises the role played by work in the processes of integration. In the industrial society, work was the main orientation point, in reference to which all other life pursuits could be planned and ordered and was valued for maintaining self-esteem and for the sense of stable social identity it offered (Giddens, 1991; Bauman, 1998: 17).

Bauman (2001) claims that the processes of globalisation and individualisation have radically transformed the physical reality of paid work in many industrialised nations. Working lives have become 'saturated with uncertainty', an uncertainty far different from the past that divides instead of uniting and there is no telling who might wake up in what division. Fears, anxieties and grievances are made in such a way as to be suffered alone, they do not add up, they do not coagulate in a common home. All this makes a solidarity-based attitude no longer a sensible choice (p 24). Giddens (2007) notes that job insecurity is not only a fear of redundancy: workers in many different types of occupation feel that they are losing control over important features of their job, such as pace of work and confidence in their overall career progression; opportunities for collaborative relations and to participate in shared activities are decreasing. Flexibility is more likely to be associated with poorly paid jobs with few career prospects.

Beck noted that the individualised society means the end of normal jobs and the end of the normal family. In the first modernity, work integrated us into society and provided us with an occupational and class position. Work was the tacit legitimation for social inequality. It determined a great deal of our consumption options and our chances to participate. With the end of full employment society, these causal chains are becoming more difficult to construct. Today, work has been 'flexibilised', and cut into spatial, temporal and contractual packets. Work loses its capacity to socialise and unemployment is parcelled out and individualised (Beck and Willms, 2004: 155–156).

As we will see in the next chapter, recent economic crises have increased the job precarity and the economic deprivation of two very large social groups. One has lost the dynamics of global competition in the past years: manual workers, the lower middle class, the unemployed and those with a temporary job. For the other group, economic crises have changed the living conditions of a large portion of the global professional class, introducing further conditions of uncertainty and reducing their income. In recent years these segments have been supporting movements for making the strategies of public regulation of the labour market more feasible and more effective in addressing the social and economic consequences of precarious work and vulnerability (Beck and Willms, 2004: 155–156). It is not clear to what extent flexible work can provide the secure foundations that an individual existence needs to flourish, not simply because it offers people a certain level of material security. If the work system begins to dissolve, how can we create an alternative milieu in which individuals who have been fragmented and atomised can be socialised? (Beck and Willms, 2004: 158).

Towards a society of isolated monads?

During the last few decades, much research has highlighted significant changes in collective values and people's willingness to relate positively with others. Families and informal networks, collaborative and care relationships of households with formal services, support networks, community organisations and social movements that represent the strength of 'the social universe' are fragmented and increasingly less relevant. Actions made by people who wish to act cooperatively as members of the same collective appear too fragile as relationships of support and care, and too often they fail to deliver well-being.

Bauman's conception of late modernity or 'liquid modernity' is pessimistic and sceptical on positive consequences of the intensification of individualisation and globalisation on individuals, families and societies on the whole. Instead of referring to modernity and postmodernity, to first and second modernity, Bauman writes of a transition from solid modernity to a more liquid form of social life characterised by constant mobility and change in relationships and identities. Forms of modern life may differ in quite a few respects – but what unites them all is precisely their fragility, temporariness, vulnerability and inclination to constant change. Flexibility has replaced solidity as the ideal condition to be pursued of things and affairs (Bauman, 2000). Precariousness, instability and vulnerability are the most widespread characteristics (and the most painfully perceived) of the condition of contemporary life; there is little that can be considered stable and reliable in the world (Bauman, 2000). But in a fully unstable context, there still is an increasing gap between individuality as destiny and individuality as a practical self-assertive skill, between the individual with his own resources and energies and the human being that has no other choice (Bauman, 2001). All 'identities', from the top to bottom, are viewed as fluid, transient and simultaneously universally available and easily lost if not individually taken care of. We do not know how much the situation we find in our life, the position we occupy, will last. In contemporary modernity human life is liquid, under constant change and transformation; in the past it was solid, and permanent. The individual becomes an isolated monad always looking for new models of sociability based on individualism.

Bauman argues that a gap is growing between individuality as fate, and individuality as the practical and realistic capacity for self-assertion (Bauman, 2001: 34). Individualisation consists of transforming human 'identity' from a 'given' into a 'task' and charging the actors with the responsibility for performing that task and for the consequences (also the side-effects) of their performance. Individualisation creates winners and losers, 'tourists' and 'vagabonds'.

> The task of self-identification has sharply disruptive side-effects. It becomes the focus of conflicts and triggers mutually incompatible drives. Since the task shared by all has to be performed by each under sharply different conditions, it divides human situations and prompts cut-throat competition rather than unifying a human condition inclined to generate co-operation and solidarity. (Bauman, 2000: 90)

Being an individual *de jure* means having no one to blame for one's own misery, seeking the causes of one's own defeats nowhere except in one's own indolence and sloth, and looking for no remedies other than trying harder and harder still. Living daily with the risk of self-reprobation and self-contempt is not an easy matter: there are, simply, no effective 'biographic solutions to systemic contradictions' (Bauman, 2001: 31–38).

The uneasiness of modernity arose from a kind of security that assigned freedom too limited a role in the pursuit of individual happiness. The uneasiness of current societies arises from a type of freedom that assigns too limited a space to individual security.

The result of individualisation is that all forms of the formal and informal association today change and take the form of swarms (aggregates without hierarchical structures, centres and command lines). By its nature, the swarm drags on aimlessly in an inconclusive way and without ever stopping for long on a meadow each time inevitably for a different reason. The swarm tends to replace the group and its leaders, hierarchy and 'pecking order'. The individual is a momentary unity of the swarm. Individualisation divides instead of uniting, and the idea of 'common interests' grows ever more nebulous and in the end becomes incomprehensible (Bauman, 2001: 24). The individual becomes an isolated monad, with weak and fragmented bonds. In the 'liquid modernity' man and woman have no permanent bonds, particularly with none of the fixed or durable bonds that would allow the effort of self-definition and self-assertion to come to a rest. These bonds must be tied loosely, so that they can be untied again, as quickly and as effortlessly as possible, when circumstances change, as they surely will in our liquid modern society (Bauman, 2003). In this setting, the prospect for a 're-embedding' of individualised actors through citizenship is dim.

Many authors argued that Bauman's methodological approach can be understood as lying 'somewhere between social science and literature': it is a 'humanistic, hybrid sociology' (Jacobsen and Marshman 2008: 798). Rattansi (2017) argues that Bauman's aversion to globalisation does not lead him to suggest any solution. Certain aspects of Bauman's ideas about liquid modernity and consumerism are useful, but he finds serious weaknesses in Bauman's interpretations of the Western modernity and globalisation (Rattansi, 2017).

In the public debate, many political and social subjects see individualisation as a danger to society and individuality itself. They emphasise the findings of much research and mainly the negative outcomes of individualism, globalisation, neoliberalism and national populism. A dazzling variety of terms has been suggested to refer to this long-lasting transition, a few of which refer positively to the emergence of a new type of social system but most of them suggest that a preceding state of affairs is drawing to a close (Giddens, 1991: 2). In fact, feelings of disorientation experienced by many political subjects make us wonder whether underlining a series of 'ends' – the end of modernity, the end of history, the end of society, the end of capitalism and so on – is not simply a reflection of this disorientation (Giddens, 1991: 98; 2007). Beck and Lau (2005: 552) suggest that what public debate and a segment of sociologists understood as 'decay', 'anomie' and 'atomised society' can be conceptualised and analysed as a moment of potential restructuration and reconceptualisation in the theoretical perspective of reflexive modernisation.

We are living in an ambivalent condition

Bauman saw individualisation as a divisive force and as a danger to society and individuality itself. Parsons and other authors represent individualisation as a consequence of a functional process of differentiation that recreates the social system through a linear one. Elias and Beck place themself between these two extreme views. Any generalisation that seeks to understand individualised society only in terms of one extreme or the other – autonomy or anomie – does not grasp the ambivalent, hybrid and contradictory character of society.

While for Bauman individualisation produces a decline of social integration, Elias claims that individualisation in the long term is an integrating force which strengthens webs of interdependence between one individual and another and their functional dependency (Elias, 2001: 129).

> With each transition from a less populous, less complex form of the dominant survival organisation to a more populous and complex one, the position of individual people in relation to the social unit they form together is changed in a characteristic way. If one attempted to present the direction of this change in a somewhat simplified form to make it amenable to more detailed investigation, one might say that the breakthrough to a new dominant form of more complex and comprehensive type of human organisation goes hand in hand with a further shift and a different pattern of individualisation. (Elias, 2001: 167–168)

Elias states that individualisation is an ambivalent process. A higher level of individualisation in its members opens the way to specific forms of fulfilment and specific forms of dissatisfaction, specific chances of happiness and contentment for individuals and specific forms of unhappiness and discomfort that are no less society-specific. More freedom of choice and more risk go together (Elias, 2001: 129).

Beck also writes of 'institutionalised individualism' but, unlike Parsons, believes that it is a non-linear, open-ended, highly ambivalent, ongoing process. Whereas for Parsons, this process remains socially stabilising, for

Beck, it has a socially transformative potential that undermines society's basic systems and institutions (Sørensen and Christiansen, 2013: 58). Many societies are not able to institutionalise an individualism functional to their needs.

Beck, according to Elias, argues that individualisation involves both the differentiation of one individual from another and integration into society (Beck and Beck-Gernsheim, 2001: xxi). He describes the three dimensions of an 'ahistorical model of individualisation' (Beck, 1992: 128): disembedding, removal from historically prescribed social forms and commitments in the sense of the traditional context of dominance and support (the 'liberating dimension'); the loss of traditional security, regarding practical knowledge, faith and guiding norms (the 'disenchantment dimension'); re-embedding, a new type of social commitment (the 'control' or 'reintegration dimension'). The process of individualisation can be understood as an ongoing social one of 'disembedding', 'disenchantment', 'reintegration' and 'control'. Individualisation is a process of transformation of social structures, collective bonds; it is the disintegration of the certainties of industrial society as well as the compulsion to find and invent new certainties for oneself. The traditional family has fallen under the normative horizon of reciprocal individualisation, which has changed private life into an open-ended experimental situation, partly voluntary, and partly against our will (Beck and Wilms, 2004: 69–70; Beck and Wilms, 2004: 69–70).

Individualisation describes a change in the relation of the individual to society. Everyone is individualised, regardless of whether they want to be or not or have the resources and basic capacities to meet the 'institutional demand for individualisation'. The generalisation of the individualisation process confronts us with the problem of generalising basic security. There is a distinction between an individualisation that takes place on the basis of system of social security and family-based mutual assistance, and an individualisation that takes place when the collective systems for providing such security are being dismantled (Beck and Wilms, 2004: 81–83). The 'do-it-yourself biography' can easily become a 'breakdown biography' depending on the economic situation, educational qualifications, stage of life, family situation and so on (Beck-Beck Gernsheim, 2001: 7). A new distribution of possibilities is simultaneously a new distribution of impossibilities for someone else. Individualisation not only multiplies side-effects, it deepens asymmetries (Beck et al, 2003: 25).

The age of the self-determined life is produced by a dense fabric of institutions (law, education, the labour market, welfare, informal relationships and so on) (Beck and Beck Gernshein, 2001: 163), and these spheres of life can render the individualisation increasingly fraught or increasingly secure. Individualisation may or may not relate to the rise of individualism or a generalisation of *homo oeconomicus*. Radical individualism does not mean a society of radically egoistic monads: individualism and social morality can be harmonised in a radically new way that Beck calls 'altruistic individualism' (Beck and Willms, 2004: 77–78).

Returning to more traditional social ties?

These authors highlighted the growing risks that accompany the middle class's individualised living conditions and the side-effects of the processes of individualisation. Several studies documented the contradictory aspect of this long-lasting transition whose direction and duration are difficult to identify as well as its possible ending points. A considerable amount of literature highlights that, in many cases, the loosening of social ties and relationships, family instability, and deregulation of the work system fail to promote a more open way of life. There are relatively few studies that support a dramatic vision of modernity or the hypothesis of an irreversible decomposition of institutions and social actors' networks towards a society of isolated monad. Much of the current literature, starting from different theoretical premises, pointed out that individualisation is a highly ambivalent process that is founded on fragile and very contradictory security conditions.

We cannot counter individualisation processes. However, a less inclusive work system, the weakening of the welfare and of the collaborative and care relationships are not unavoidable effects of individualisation. These critical issues highlight, instead, the difficulties that contemporary societies encounter in creating new forms of system and social reintegration, less fragile and less contradictory security conditions.

Over the last two decades, the effects of unstable relationships permeate every sphere of life, from work to family relations. The evolution of the labour market has exposed the majority of people to income changes, which the family and other social networks often fail to compensate for with the same efficacy previously experienced; precarious work and precarious relationships are often intertwined. Individualisation has liberated people from traditional roles and constraints, but these have come at the expense of undermining intermediate institutions and collective life patterns. Equally, austerity and welfare retrenchment play a critical role. The welfare state provided the basis of relative social security (the provision of education, unemployment benefits and universal health coverage) for an intensification of individualisation. These processes contributed both to the transformation of the foundations of common life and to the stabilisation of these ways of life (Beck and Beck-Gernsheim, 2001). In last two decades, the welfare state can, only with increasing difficulty, guarantee social and economic security – protection from poverty, precarity and unemployment, sickness and old age; a minimum income; social, health and pension benefits – through which the individuals can build their individual projects for the future and somehow protect their day-to-day living.

This awareness can help us rethink the forms of sociality and the social bonds that we can build to find the conditions to support people's autonomy and individual life projects within a widely shared system of value and norms. Individualisation is imposed by the main institutions that often cannot address the major social challenges of individualised society, ensuring the radical risks of the second modernity and improving the quality of their relationship with citizens.

Again, it is necessary to carefully observe the changes in the work system, welfare and ordinary human relationships. New forms of aggregation and new cultures of human relations are emerging together with relationships that have a regressive dimension. In European societies, in the midst of the COVID-19 pandemic, a huge debate emerged about the increase in resignation rates among mid-level employees and the shift in priorities and attitudes and the role of work in people's lives (called the Great Resignation). The pandemic has also promoted social support relationships in the context of extended kinship, the neighbourhood, close friendships, and in building new forms of association between families. The pandemic has reopened the public debate on the need to build efficient universalistic welfare, to strengthen the role of the state, territorial health services, social and preventive activities, with the awareness that in the spread of many pathologies, not only infectious ones, individual health depends on collective health (Pierson, 2021; Siza, 2021 and 2022).

Another change mainly concerns the relationship between the generations within the family and the independence of the youngest members. In countries like Italy and Portugal, relations and ties between young adults and the family of origin appear to be considerably stronger than in the past, inverting the seemingly irreversible trend towards individuality and conflictual estrangement from the family. In many cases, these new behaviours and attitudes have a regressive character and constitute a return to more traditional equilibrium within the families and an attenuation of generational conflict. Many others simply recognise that the emotional value of proximal relationships can enrich an individual project and independent life.

Conclusion

A long-lasting transition towards a second modern society continuously creates new economic and social risk and cultural changes which simultaneously are producing a progressive erosion of three pillars of the system and social integration of contemporary Western societies: family and informal relations, work, and welfare. Undoubtedly, all three pillars have progressively lost their integrative capacity, and within them, the sources of risk have grown. Castel (2003: xvi) believes that the precariousness of the jobs can be compensated by the density of the networks of social protection offered by the family, neighbours and other informal relations. Somers states that we are in an era of market fundamentalism where prevails the drive to subject civil sphere and the public sphere to market mechanisms (2008: 2).

In the following chapters, I explore the new and old social divisions rising in Western Europe and the responses of welfare systems. I also argue that it is possible to counter the dynamic that weakens sociality, collective actions and relations of mutual support. It is possible to identify the conditions required to strengthen the system and social integration, improve the inclusive capacity of work, and reproduce care and collaborative relationships through welfare system resources.

The individualisation process is a case of 'institutionalised individualisation': to some extent, a constraint, a forced execution of market requirements imposed on the individual by modern institutions, and it is a desire and an opportunity that releases people from the constraints of tradition. The issue is that individualisation is socially produced, but socialisation institutions such as the education system and family, in my view, are still too weak. Contemporary European societies create active individualism but fail to institutionalise a kind of individualism functional for their growth.

Such theorists of individualisation as Parsons, Bauman and Beck have coined several terms to describe the emerging social order: 'second modernity', 'high modernity' and 'liquid modernity'. They highlight that radical processes are transforming the basic institutions of society, from the family to the institutional order, not only households' income, work and economic life.

In this chapter I argued that the main institutions encounter increasing difficulty facing these changes and creating new forms of system and social integration. Welfare is considered an essential resource of the processes of integration, but social and political subjects do not always grasp its potential. In many cases, they promote a welfare that accompanies a development and a kind of individualisation deemed linear and inevitable with only incremental changes to its organisation. In others, they can consider that collaborative and care resources are destined to gradually disappear in a society of the isolated monad, thus accepting that only market or public resources truly matter in building a welfare state. Finally, in a third direction, institutions recognise the ambivalences and opportunities of this long-lasting transition and mobilise the care and social inclusion resources that every sphere of life (informal relations, welfare, work system) can ensure.

3

The rise of a new 'middle mass'

A new politically and socially unstable stratum

A large part of the middle class has lost a variety of certainties relating to family and informal relations, the functioning of public institutions, and is also exposed to similar uncertainties in other systems of social integration, such as work and welfare. A great deal of previous research has documented the loss of economic security and the uncertainty created by the fast change in cultural values such as multiculturalism, open borders, acceptance of gender and racial equality. In my view, to explain the emerging radical activism, resentment against institutions, and a culture of fear against non-traditional lifestyles, immigrants and foreigners requires us to focus on several other factors. As we argued in previous chapters, there is a 'multiple determination' of a single event (Pawson and Tilley, 1997; Bhaskar, 2008); the interactions of causal relations existing in every context shape the economic and social disadvantages of several social groups. An individualised context can hinder or increase the generative capacity of the causal relationship such as relative deprivation and cultural backlash. Research on the intensification of individualisation and on the transition towards the second modernity can shed more light on a more general process and the social setting in which these economic and cultural dynamics develop.

The central focus of the chapter is the crisis of the kind of individualism of people who compete in relatively ordered ways and abide by the rules and institutions that they contribute to creating through their own personal commitment and autonomy. As we have seen in the previous chapters, first Parsons (1937; 1978), then Elias (1991) and Beck (1992) and Beck and Beck-Gernsheim (1995; 2001) called this kind of individualism 'institutionalised individualism'. This individualism is oriented by norms and values and forms the functioning of the central institutions of society.

Western societies are no longer able to promote a kind of individualism functional to the improvement of society and the inclusion of relevant social groups in an active society. Beck states that individualisation is accompanied by a uniformity of form of living: such individualisation delivers people over an external control and standardisation that was unknown in the enclaves of familial and feudal sub-cultures (Beck, 1992: 132). In my view, the critical point is that social differentiation processes are becoming less functional and stronger than every standardisation process and continually conflict with them. These processes try to prevail on systemic imperative, creating a continuous tension in every sphere of life such as work system, welfare, intimate relationships.

In this chapter, I argue that the intensification of individualisation in all European countries is contributing to creating a new politically and socially unstable stratum at the centre of the social stratification. This is a multitude of active and reflexive individuals, with weak collective ties that voice radical activism that institutions are progressively less able to manage. They are not individuals and households involved in dynamics of severe poverty but people experiencing other several critical dynamics: the impact of a market polarisation, growing precarity, increased competition and a weakening of the informal networks of support and the public welfare institutions. Social groups that do not live at the margins of society, in separate territorial and social areas, are not socially isolated but take part in social life though in constant insecurity about the conditions reached from time to time. The working conditions expose them inevitably to sudden fluctuations of income, and in other spheres of life, they experience similar precariousness. Rather than a 'break up' of social ties produced by processes of exclusion, the most important dynamics of this condition is an accumulation of many insecurities in many spheres of life.

At the bottom of the social structure

In all Western European countries, welfare systems are changing to address the demographic crisis, promoting work–life balance, and the financial sustainability of the health and pension systems. Welfare states have changed even more profoundly to address two emerging crises that directly involve the attitudes and behaviours of low-income households. The first crisis has to do with the belief that 'dangerous' classes are emerging at the margin of society. Since the 1990s, several studies have emphasised the problematic social integration of a multitude of individuals; groups which for a long time have been at the margins of the labour market and in many cases are characterised by high crime rates and drug and alcohol addiction. In many European countries such as the Netherlands, the United Kingdom and France, a considerable amount of research has highlighted the emergence of the 'underclass', a dangerous class for morally reprehensible behaviour and detachment from the standards of civil society. People of the underclass are deemed 'the irresponsible poor', threatening the safety of communities and societal cohesion. The public debate emphasises the need for increased surveillance, behavioural restrictions and punitive actions to avoid the collapse of the family and the disintegration of Western societies. A punitive welfare system and the increased expansion of the penal state are gradually shaping the daily life of this urban poor segment.

The second crisis refers to the need to govern and address benefit claimants' passivity, the welfare dependency of many low-income families, the long-term unemployed, and ordinary individuals living in deprived areas. As we will see in the next chapter, welfare conditionality is the main attempt of European welfare states to discipline welfare recipients and regulate the conduct of low-income populations through punitive policies, penalties or 'sanctions'. These policies are designed to reduce or suspend welfare benefits. In a shared perspective of social crime prevention and 'zero tolerance' and 'broken windows', this irregular behaviour can lead people to commit crimes and become dangerous to the social order.

Much research found a significant correlation between areas with deprivation in terms of education, income and employment, and support for anti-establishment parties, radical movements, and protests for essential goods and destructive actions (Armingeon and Ceka, 2013; Funke et al, 2016; Algan et al, 2017; Becker et al, 2017). Other research highlight the precarious integration of these social groups. Castel points out the growing presence of individuals who virtually drift within the social structure and populate interstices of society without finding any established position within it:

> Vague silhouettes, at the margins of labour and at the frontiers of socially consecrated forms of exchange – the long-time unemployed, inhabitants of abandoned suburbs, recipients of a national minimum income, victims of industrial downsizing, young people in search of employment who carry themselves from place to place, from menial jobs to temporary work – who are these people, where did they come from, and what will become of them? (Castel, 2003: xv)

Although youth from the inner cities or deprived neighbourhoods are not outside, excluded from society, they nevertheless do not occupy any recognisable place within, with many seemingly not able to get one (Castel, 2007). Castel introduces the term 'negative individualism'. In other words, that individualism is obtained by subtracting from community ties, unlike the individualism of modernity, which means the enhancement of the subject and independence from general groups (2003).

Guy Standing (2011; 2014) focuses his analysis on 'the precariat', a class-in-the-making in his definition, comprising marginal population segments. This class consists of millions of people subject to flexible, insecure labour relations and is rapidly becoming a mass of workers in contemporary countries. It is a class without an anchor and which is creating instability within society.

In his influential research Standing argues that the growing precarity and polarisation of the labour market is particularly devasting for three groups. The first consists of people removed from working-class communities and families. Their parents or grandparents belonged to working-class occupations that had status, skill and respect (Standing, 2014: 29). The second consists of migrants, Roma, ethnic minorities, asylum seekers, some disabled, and a growing number of ex-convicts. This group, too, experiences relative deprivation. The nostalgia may be delusional, but anger is likely combined with a pragmatic need to survive. This part of the precariat may be detached from the political and social mainstream (Standing, 2014: 29). The third, the dynamic core of the precariat, consists of the educated, who have been plunged into a precariat existence after being promised the opposite: a bright career of personal development and satisfaction. Most are in their twenties and thirties, yet they are not alone. Many drifting out of a salariat existence are joining them. The defining feature of this part of the precariat is another form of relative deprivation, a sense of status frustration (Standing, 2014: 30). In brief, the first part of the precariat experiences deprivation relative to a real or imagined past, the second relative to an absent present, an absent 'home', and the third relates to a feeling of having no future. The combination of anxiety, alienation, anomie and anger can be expected to lead to more days of riot and protest. Standing (2011) argues that the 'precariat' is the 'new dangerous class' because they are increasingly frustrated and angry and are prone to listen to ugly voices and use their votes and money to give those voices a political platform of increasing influence (p 1).

In my view, the 'precariat' is not a class-in-the-making. Increasing precariousness involves its contextualisation since it has very different effects on different individuals. Nevertheless, many authors often observe precariousness in deterministic terms. They do not often explore its implications on downward and upward social mobility; the very broad articulation of social destinies it contributes to creating. As Bourdieu (2001) states, precariousness is everywhere, and it tends to expand every relational sphere. However, its effects on people's lives are very different. For some, this condition is a destiny of insecurity; it degrades the relationship with the world, with time, and with space; for others, it extends the opportunity of social mobility out of proportion. An unstable life can ensure fast processes of upwards social mobility or a worsening of their living conditions. When it has a multidimensional character that involves many spheres of life, it weighs with particular force upon those parts of the lowest segments of the labour market. For example, a divorce creates additional challenges for non-standard workers while self-employees with better income have more resources to cover a similar event.

Other scholars recognise the role of the precariat in anti-austerity mobilisations and in global justice movements as the new agents of protest in a time of austerity (Della Porta, 2015; G. Martin, 2015). People are motivated to become involved in collective action by emotions such as anger, indignation and a sense of injustice (G. Martin, 2015: 3). These protests are in reaction to the economic crisis and the political situation in which the institutions exist. They 'reflect the pauperisation of the lower classes as well as the proletarianisation of the middle classes, with the growth of the excluded in some countries to about two-thirds of the population' (Della Porta, 2015: 35).

For many authors, below the 'precariat' there is another 'dangerous class': the 'old underclass', which refers to vulnerable African American people marked by chronic poverty and detached from common values. Moreover, a new 'white underclass' has been emerging over the last two decades (Murray, 2013; Case and Deaton, 2020): wage rates are declining for less educated Whites and workers of this class are reacting either by withdrawing from the market or by taking worse jobs. Case and Deaton (2020) point to a growing social polarisation between the college educated, who are becoming healthier and wealthier, and those without a college degree, who are subject to increasingly harsh conditions of life. In this account, those left behind perceive the system to be rigged against them, while at the same time locating the fault for such disparity within themselves. The combination of these two things leads to resentment:

> Declining wages are part of the story, but we believe that it is impossible to explain despair through declining material advantage. We believe that much more important for despair is the decline of family, community, and religion. These declines may not have happened without the decline in wages and in quality of jobs that made traditional working class life possible. But it was the destruction of a way of life that we see as central, not the decrease in material wellbeing; wages work through these factors, not directly. (Case and Deaton, 2020: 183)

In many respects, what happened to African Americans in the 1960s, is now happening to the White working class in the US and in Europe. The social institutions – family, community, welfare – no longer provide support and sustenance. The old and new 'underclass' have a marginal position in the labour market, similar to other disadvantaged groups. However, their economic position is reinforced by their social confinement in segregated areas of cities, increasingly isolated from the more affluent part of the Black and White communities, from the world of employment, from the institutions, and from the set of relations that can help their members to come out of poverty (Wilson, 1987; Case and Deaton, 2020).

At the centre of social stratification

The growing precarity of the labour market and the weakening of the informal support networks are particularly devastating for certain working-class segments. However, these struggles no longer only concern the working class, the 'precariat' and the old and new 'underclass' who are neither reliable workers nor reliable consumers – for which every process of individualisation has meant economic and social fractures. Unstable and fluid conditions can also be found outside these social groups, even among more established social positions. It encompasses the rapidly growing number of working- and middle-class individuals facing economic and social insecurity.

Not only the poor segments of the working class (the precariat) are affected. The White working class is not a homogeneous group and is varied as any other group in society. The other two segments (the traditional working class; the emergent service workers) (Savage et al, 2015: 240–243; Beider, 2015) express, often in very different and more incisive forms, a profound distrust of major social and political institutions and ensure support for radical parties. The recurrent economic crises involve several social groups, not only the most deprived ones. The weakening of the inclusive nature of the work system and the informal networks of support no longer ensure a relatively stable integration for most people.

These changes have emphasised all the ambivalence and social risks of the processes of individualisation and have dramatically reduced the opportunities for a considerable share of the population to construct their future in autonomy. The same is happening to the middle class. In the last two decades, only a small segment of this class has registered an improvement in their living conditions by gaining entry to the established middle class (Savage et al, 2015), and a segment by becoming part of the global professional class. On the other hand, the vast majority of middle-class households have seen their living conditions worsen, having lost certainties related to work stability and income. Social and economic divides are growing between the latter and the former.

Moreover, the distinction between the large part of the middle class and the working class in terms of social identity, income, consumption and quality of work is decreasing. For these groups in the middle of the social stratification, it is difficult to draw clear boundaries compared to each class's specific economic, social and cultural capital; there is a degree of convergence between segments of the middle class and working class (Crompton, 2008; Savage et al, 2015).

Recent studies have attempted to highlight the relative importance of the working class, and the larger part of the middle class (without considering the 'upper middle class') in their active support for anti-establishment parties (for example, Becker et al, 2017; Dorling and Tomlinson, 2020).

Therefore, it is not easy to grasp the social basis of many protests, such as street demonstrations and radical electoral behaviours. Populism appeals to a broad alliance of different groups in society (Eatwell and Godwin, 2018: 17). In many peripheral rural areas, the working class is not numerically large, and it is joined by a large number of former members of the middle class. However, due to their lack of specialised or higher education, the working class is much more vulnerable. In these areas, these two groups form a new minority that no longer expects anything from the authorities and feel that they have nothing left to lose (Muzergues, 2020: 46–47). In other ones, the 'amalgam' involves more segments of the middle and working class (Jetten et al, 2020). Antonucci et al's findings reject the dichotomous view of the low-educated 'Brexiter' versus the highly-educated 'Remainer', by showing that two groups with intermediate levels of education were more pro-leave than the low-educated. The 'Leave' vote is associated with self-identification as middle class, and the more neutral 'no class' identification. They find no evidence of a link with working-class identification (Antonucci et al, 2017).

Therefore, we should pay more attention to this 'amalgam' involving more middle- and working-class segments, groups with 'intermediate levels of education' and with 'no class self-identification'. I believe that within a context featured by radical processes of individualisation, we can better understand the blurring boundaries between them and the emerging difference and similarities between these groups. Rather than a dramatic upheaval of social strata, the rising proliferation of unstable relations throughout all life domains produces marked effects on numerous intermediate social groups.

In my view, in many countries of Western Europe, there has been a growth of an extended social stratum formed by the majority (a large part of the middle and working classes), which is separated and increasingly distanced from the upper-middle-class and low-income households. This extended social stratum feels, to various degrees, that they are in a shared condition of economic difficulty, lacking security, status and trust in the future. However, they represent a non-structured social stratum, a non-homogeneous aggregation, with internal divisions and a frail collective identity.

This stratum is similar to Wilensky's (1975: 118–119; 2002) 'middle mass' which also included the upper working class and the lower middle class. In Wilensky's classification, the lower middle class was a very large class consisting of semi-technical, semi-professional occupational clerks (for example, laboratory technicians), school teachers, cashiers, salespeople, nurses and so forth. An increasing portion of the self-employed, small business entrepreneurs, craft workers and consultants became an integral part of the middle mass. The upper working class mainly consisted of manual workers in the building trade, trucking, and craft workers.

Wilensky's 'middle mass' was a product of a process of individualisation of the first modernity that has only partially eroded traditional affiliation (church, union, voluntary association). The new 'middle mass' is mainly a product of a process of individualisation of the second modernity. The intensification of this process has weakened every form of belonging and social ties, has freed people from traditional roles and constraints and undermined 'intermediate institutions' such as trade unions, political parties, ethnic groups and collective organisations. However, the dissolving of roles, ties and old institutions only for some segments means an open way of life and more freedom.

Unlike Wilensky's middle mass, the new middle mass has to face processes of radical individualisation that have made old and new forms of sociality unstable, fragmented group homogeneity, overlapped new and old values and beliefs. The new 'middle mass' is a sort of a multitude characterised by radical activism, a multitude of active individuals experiencing relative economic deprivation to varying degrees. Every deprivation is experienced mostly individually and is perceived and dealt with by individuals with weaker social networks. Work was not more valued for the sense of stable social identity that it ensured; every collective strategy to sustain a kind of institutionalised individualism has become obsolete and has lost some of its importance.

In 1970s, the middle mass was formed of a multitude of passive people, manipulated by mass media and consumption imperatives, becoming more alike in lifestyle, behaviour and political outlook. The citizen of the middle mass worked hard at a disciplined job. He struggled for a decent and safe house, higher wages, greater safety and freedom on the job, and a full range of consumer goods (Wilensky, 1975: 117). Industrialisation shaped stratification and mobility:

> [I]t blurs older class lines, creates increasing social, cultural and political heterogeneity within each social class such that internal differences within classes become greater than differences between them; and it fosters the emergence of a politically restive 'middle mass' (upper-working-class, lower-middle class) whose behavior, values, beliefs, and tastes increasingly differ from those of the privileged college-educated upper-middle class and the very rich above them and the poor below. (Wilensky, 2002: 679)

The revolt of the middle mass against the welfare expressed in those years was linked to the growing social and cultural distance between this stratum and the poor and the growing tax burden and its high social visibility (Wilensky, 1976). The multiple economic crises of the mid-1970s intensified the competition between natives and foreigners in the Netherlands, the UK, West Germany and France (Wilensky, 1975: 58).

Wilensky argued that the increasing influence of mass media in many Western countries had eroded civil society, primary groups such as the family and neighbourhood, and self-governing associations such as unions and the church. The decline and the increasingly superficial quality of civic engagement did not contribute to developing ties to communities and society. The breakdown of traditional political structures and major interest groups (especially labour, employers, professionals, farmers) was a real threat to democracy and the social order (Wilensky, 1961; 2002). As rich countries became richer, the middle mass as a political force became more fluid, torn loose from traditional political identities, and more strategic, larger and more influential as a swing vote (Wilensky, 1975: 116).

The cleavage of the new 'middle mass'

The current extended social stratum encompasses many of the social groups of Wilensky's middle mass. However, the new segments of the middle and working classes have economic conditions, lifestyles, attitudes towards welfare and main institutions, increasingly different from the established middle class, and to the more disadvantaged segments of the precariat and people in persistent poverty. Moreover, many significant differences have emerged in terms of economic security and opportunities between the lower middle and other segments of the upper middle classes (Goldthorpe and McKnight, 2004).

Over the past two decades, this separation has become more marked in many Western European countries. Among the social groups that constitute this stratum, the traditional class divisions are being eased: the divide between the middle and working class that underpinned class analysis since its foundation in the thinking of Marx and Weber, is becoming less and less clear (Grusky and Weisshaar, 2014; Savage, 2015; Savage et al, 2015).

The new 'middle mass' is a heterogeneous entity despite having shared values and concerns, and several non-secondary living conditions in common, such as a perception of being an economically 'left behind' group, detached from institutions and elites, with low likelihood of improving their income position, and low opportunities of upward social mobility. The progressive erosion of the inclusive capacity of the three pillars of the system and social integration of contemporary societies (family and informal relations, work, and welfare) has increased its uncertainty. A combination of socioeconomic uncertainties, fragilities, vulnerabilities and constant activism affects the quality and the direction of their life relations and collective activities and expectations. For many years, it was believed that anyone could independently manage their own personal growth, obtaining advantages and higher degrees of freedom than those obtainable in a static society, in which individuals are forced to abide by traditional obligations and live stable relationships with little possibility of change in the short term. The situation has changed dramatically over the last 20 years, and the balances between individual risks (unemployment, precarity, instability and loosening of informal ties) and growth opportunities seem to have disappeared. The forms of individualism promoted by many societies have become increasingly risky and dysfunctional, leading to the loss of numerous opportunities to fulfil life plans and hopes on which the 'institutionalised individualism' advocated by Parsons was based.

This extended social stratum has a fluid social identity for the simultaneous flexibilisation of work, family and all social rights, the latter caused by enhancing the politics of privatisation and welfare retrenchment. Digital technology and 'social media' rather than traditional mass media are shaping the lives of its members. The networks of online and offline relationships built within its members provide a sense of belonging and relative security, and a shared temporary social identity. The large utilisation of new digital media strengthens models of sociability based on individualism and provides adequate material support for the spread of individualism as the dominant form of social relations (Castells, 2001: 129). The response to the frailty of human bonds is found in replacing quality in our relations for quantity (Bauman, 2003).

Instead of individualism as a way to achieve their own life project, this type of individualism grows losing essential links to the work system and other spheres of life.

The recurrent economic crisis has increased the insecurity and the economic deprivation of two segments of this social stratum and produced new lines of social division. New divisions emerge between the losers and the winners of globalisation and all social classes (middle class, global middle class, working class, the bottom of the social stratification). On the one hand, these crises have further affected the living conditions of those who have lost within the dynamics of globalisation: manual workers, the lower middle class, the unemployed and those in temporary employment. On the other, they have changed the living conditions of a large portion of the most dynamic and globalised individuals, who have improved their income thanks to the opening of commercial trade and professional relationships that globalisation has ensured.

In recent years, global economic trends have reduced their economic resources, introducing further elements of uncertainty and caution, thereby weakening their life projects, and the values that underpin their worldviews. For many, recurrent crises such as the economic and climate, the intensification of globalisation, and the COVID-19 pandemic have dissolved securities and life projects, highlighting the growing risks that accompany individualised living conditions. They can be members of that social group defined as the 'creative class' (Florida, 2012) whose members' work is constituted by a significant creative component (intellectual professions such as healthcare practitioners and technical occupations, university professors and high school teachers, lawyers). Similarly, members of the global middle class who live in different European countries share knowledge, customs, cultural references and life projects but experience very different basic security and welfare state resources in their home countries.

These segments of the middle and working classes constitute a deep new social division that is altering the structure of the middle of the social stratification and tends to produce a shared social identity and increase its internal cohesion. Class identification, the extent to which they identify themselves as middle- and working-class members, is still robust, but it becomes blurred in collective actions and voting behaviours.

In all Western European countries, this division constitutes the social structural base of a new cleavage that weakens traditional left–right cleavages based on the working class (left-wing political parties) or in the middle class (conservative parties). For many authors (Lipset and Rokkan, 1967; Bartolini and Mair, 1990; Kriesi, 1998; Badie et al, 2011; Bartolini, 2011) the notion of a cleavage includes three essential elements: a social-structural element, a sense of collective identity and the willingness to organise durable collective actions. This term identifies social and political divisions characterised by a close connection between the positioning of individuals in terms of social stratification, their beliefs and normative orientations, and behavioural patterns. This close connection contributes to the stability of cleavages over time.

In this new cleavage, a shared set of cultural attitudes, beliefs and values grow that quite often are against the establishment and political institutions. Over the last two decades, this cleavage has expressed shared values and expectations that constitute the basis for the organisation of relevant interests, for individual and collective activism that ensures support and ties with radical parties and shapes their priorities. The relative economic deprivation and cultural backlash are often 'contingent trigger events' that reveal crisis, further worsen their precarious living conditions, and fuel radical collective activism and unpredictable voting choices.

The social basis of cleavages that fuel protests are not just the poor and the 'dangerous classes'. These social divisions have a weak structure and a fluid social basis and are not able to form the basis for large mass identification. These political and social minorities can represent new worrying social fragmentation, which can fuel local movements for single issues (actions for collective benefits, such as the fight against local pollution) quite often separate from the protests of the majority of people. Wider societal grievance, activism and street protests tend to overrepresent the middle class while individuals from resource-poor groups are most likely to be politically disengaged (Evans and Tilley, 2015; 2017; Giugni and Grasso, 2019).

The new 'middle mass' has the social and cultural resources to bring together in collective movements both the social resentment of the precariat and the new uncertainties of the mass of the middle and working classes. The number of people taking part in these collective protests is increasing in Western Europe. In most cases, these protests are likely to become a normal means of political participation, normalising protests and protesters

(Van Aelst and Walgrave, 2001). At times, more radical groups spiral out of control and can fuel violent protests, leading to property damage and looting (Jetten et al, 2020).

In Western Europe, the new 'middle mass' is not only disenchanted with major social and political institutions but what prevails among its members is an active radical individualism which is less and less integrated and beyond the control of institutions. This kind of individualism seems to be increasingly less socialised to the rules and objectives of a society that aims at competitiveness and fosters individual initiative.

Within this cleavage, confidence in institutions, civic values and trust in other people are declining, undermining any kinds of 'institutionalised individualism' as a founding social principle of Western societies. In parallel to the 'institutionalised individualism' of Parsons and Beck, other kinds of individualism and 'survival strategies' are emerging. Ones in which a mass of individuals put together radically different values and ways of life, which are neither regulated nor easily manageable and are characterised by a confusing array of aspirations, resentments and intolerance towards rules and institutions. This active discontent for what one is surrounded by extends to every aspect of life: social bonds, rules and institutions. A significant segment believes that compliance with the rules is ultimately an obstacle to improving their social position. Others use online networks to interact with hate groups and take real-world actions against members of other races, different sexual orientations and religions. Many have quit voting or have a high level of electoral volatility, swinging between phases of 'dealignment' in which these groups cut the bonds with traditional parties and new phases of 'realignments' leading to the formation of new linkages with other parties (Dalton et al, 1984; Mayhew, 2000; Eatwell and Godwin, 2018: 225–253).

In short, the condition of this social stratum constitutes a significant critical 'juncture' for many societies, a condition capable of modifying social relations and social structures. As we have seen in Chapter 2, these forms of active individualism are mainly created by the radical processes of individualisation of the second modernity (Beck, 1992) that has weakened ties between individuals and their social network and has liberated people from their traditional roles and constraints. But, in so doing, these processes often do not create effective and shared forms of social reintegration.

A mass of active and reflexive individuals

At the end of the 20th century, many authors (Betz, 1994; Hainsworth, 2000) observed the rise of the 'extremism of the centre'. With the new millennium, both the numerical dimension of the radical activism of middle classes and the radicality of its collective behaviours have grown dramatically, making it harder for institutions and other spheres of life to govern these public and private actions.

In much of Western Europe, the enabling state, the family and the system of work are less and less able to manage and include a mass of active and reflexive individuals with weak collective ties. Integration in highly differentiated societies has become increasingly difficult: all European societies currently face growing difficulty in promoting individual initiative and institutionalising the utilitarian aspects of individualism. In this long-lasting transition period, the re-embedding part of individualisation is still less effective than its disembedding portion of subjects and resources (Van Loon, 2002: 33).

Democratic societies that fostered the individualisation processes are now facing kinds of individualism that are difficult to govern (Giddens, 1991; Ignazi, 2003; Siza, 2017; 2019). Many concerns of households in this cleavage arise between the need to build one's future and the sensation of living in a condition of profound uncertainty. What seems to be re-emerging among these social groups is the condition known as 'status inconsistency' whereby income, occupation and education are no longer clearly correlated (Hodge and Treiman, 1968). People understand what being middle class means in the abstract, but many find themselves in complicated positions that imply different class identities (Hout, 2008: 31–32). Differences in education, social capital or professional skills usually do not create clear social outcomes in terms of upward social mobility and higher income.

The newly acquired universes of values are no longer compatible with the instability of the employment sector, economic hardship and the fragility of their social networks. They have limited access to economic, social and cultural resources needed to face the risks of a globalised society. All of the intermediate structures, such as the nuclear family, collective belonging, collective associations and the neighbourhood, are weakened. Traditional conservative movements and other organisations such as unions that once represented middle-class households have declined. The combined degradation of the material conditions of life and a crisis of the legitimacy of institutions has induced many middle-class households to take matters into their own hands, engaging in collective action outside institutional channels. As Castells suggests (2012: 218–236), the influence of these actions on policy may appear limited at least in the short term; however, they have a much deeper and growing influence on the population at large.

In a long transition, a new kind of sociality and belonging struggles to emerge. New autonomous forms and resources of social coexistence and relations of care are emerging among people, and though they might help individuals live an independent life, at present they seem not to be able to replace traditional values and relationships. The atomisation and isolation of individuals becomes more frequent than the open and dynamic kinds of sociality that the second modernity promised. The attitudes emerging among these groups erode the ability of institutions to function and weaken civic values.

Processes of individualisation have fragmented group homogeneity and weakened the traditional and modern forms of belonging and social ties. These processes are changing the relations of the individual to society, altering the relationship of the middle class with the top and bottom layers of the social stratification, as well as its interest in supporting and defending traditional configurations of welfare. The responses of institutions to face the spread of these radical processes of individualisation have been weak or misjudged.

The individualism of the new middle mass is harder to govern also because of the social divisions between the ruling classes in their entirety and the rest. A large part of the ruling class no longer intends pursuing a proactive, mediating role in supporting institutional rules and functions. In many Western countries, those at the top feel outside of the resources that the system normally offers (state schools, public healthcare, social services), but also outside the duties and rules of the social life of the majority (Siza, 2019). The upper classes, Sassen suggests, refuse to take social responsibility, represent collective interests, act as a role model, and create limits and criteria that help distinguish between morally acceptable and morally reprehensible behaviour (2014: 15). The 'global company' is a key institution in the post-democratic world that has gained supremacy over governments, parties and politics. We are moving towards a new ruling class, which is politically and economically increasingly dependent on executives of multinational corporations and businesses (Crouch, 2004).

New social divisions, new cleavages

Many authors recognise the great divide between the 1 per cent and the 99 per cent as the biggest social threat of our time. Stiglitz (2015), Atkinson (2015) and Piketty (2014) note the dramatic increase in income disparity between 'the richest 1 per cent and the rest' and the growing concentration of wealth and income in the upper classes. In their articles, they note that the rise in the wealth of the very rich – sometimes described as the 1 per cent – has had a noticeable effect on overall income inequality in the US and other countries, particularly in Western Europe. Dorling (2015) argues that the vast majority of the 99 per cent are becoming more equal and often poorer than they were in 2008. The gap with the 1 per cent is increasing, while inequality within it has fallen.

In contrast, it is possible to argue that there are many social and economic divides within this '99 per cent' that risk remaining hidden from the analyses on extreme inequality. Undoubtedly, in European countries, there is a great divide separating the ultra-rich and the rest. However, the latter is not a homogeneous class regarding education, language, career paths and so on. Economic and demographic changes have destroyed the stable tripartite social class system (upper, middle and working). Payne (2013: 65) argues that class divisions still exist, but they are no longer easily mapped in the tripartite imagery of social classes There is more fragmentation of the class system and a transformation of traditional 'simple divisions'. Many divisions now give rise to 'compounded divides' (cleavage) that offer their members a stronger sense of belonging and security.

Western European societies appear to be characterised not only by a marked inequality, but likewise by the presence of numerous intermediate positions between the bottom and the top of the social stratification, that no longer form a system of stable relations and values on which to build social standards, a link between the parts (as the middle classes were traditionally in the past). On the contrary, these positions constitute one of the most significant critical issues for social cohesion.

The concept of separating the top 1 per cent and the rest of the population partially highlight tendencies and dynamics that are changing structural aspects of European countries. While the divides that progressively separate an extended social stratum from the established middle class and multiple disadvantaged groups are important to highlight, the values and emerging forms of belonging deserve more attention.

Within the '99 per cent', we can distinguish actual social groupings that share common living conditions – particularly in terms of income, work and relation to institutions – which are very different between them. More emphasis should be placed on how the growing concentration of wealth and income in the upper classes remake the social stratification and the different groupings that compose the working and middle classes (Butler and Savage, 1995; Crompton, 2008). Different classes, ethnic groups, genders and so on have given rise to different interests, norms about what is proper, and orientations towards social and political issues. Fragmented societies are emerging characterised by many divisions which are more or less endowed with crucial resources and more or less exposed to risks, differently placed in networks of interaction and communication (Svallfors, 2007: 9). We are witnessing the rebirth of social cleavage grounded outside the division of labour. For example, ethnicity is becoming a more important marker of belonging and identity for many groups (Svallfors, 2007: 8).

This does not imply that the upper and low middle class and working class have disappeared, leaving behind a shapeless mass of groups. We are not, therefore, as opined by Beck (1992: 88), witnessing a 'capitalism devoid of classes', nor are we only capable of observing the 'individualised fragments' of no longer relevant social classes (Beck and Beck-Gernsheim, 2001). Rather, the distinction between many social positions within many classes has been reduced considerably; they are more unstable, and at times even overlap. Family background, educational level, traditional differences in lifestyle and life projects have all lost some of their relevance but still influence life courses often in counterintuitive forms. The concept of social stratification consists of more than simply inequalities in life chances. It refers to the idea that individuals are distributed among social strata that are real social groupings, forged together through their economic and associated social relations and interactions. A social stratum connects individuals and helps build up boundaries that enclose groups and divide them from others (Scott, 2013: 29).

Conclusion

This chapter aims to contribute to ongoing public and academic debates about social and political instability. I have argued that within a landscape featured by an intensification of individualisation processes, we can understand the growing radical activism and the unpredictability of many social groups attitudes and behaviours.

In Western Europe, this radical activism involves not only just the poor and 'the precariat'. It affects a considerable part of the middle and working classes who appear less and less able to build their own life projects that would allow them to survive amidst the growing insecurity. Extensive processes have profoundly transformed their fabric of social relations and a significant part of its collective identity and membership.

Like Wilensky's middle mass, the contemporary 'middle mass' is a sort of a multitude of individuals with an unstable social identity and activism which institutions are progressively less able to manage. This extended social stratum is separated and increasingly distanced from the upper middle class and low-income households. This multitude of individuals believe in having lost the economic and social conditions needed to feel part of active society and realise their life projects through individual action and effort, respecting and re-enforcing a fair social order and civic coexistence. They are afraid that the current economic difficulty will become permanent, with little hope of increasing their income and opportunities for upward mobility in the near future.

Much research fails to acknowledge the critical role of these changes in the middle of social stratification, even though they are extremely relevant to how variations in the values and norms of civil coexistence occur and in the organisation of welfare services.

Radical activism of the middle class has eroded the ordinary capacity of existing welfare institutions, to manage and include many social groups. As will be seen in the next chapter, welfare chauvinism, conditionality and new forms of dualisation and other divisive welfare forms are misjudged responses to these changes. Many rich democracies have successfully addressed the consequences of precarious work and vulnerability by, for example, managing labour markets more effectively, re-establishing and expanding social safety nets, and implementing social and economic reforms (Kallenberg, 2018: 5).

Nonetheless, in many Western European nations, the institutions seem incapable of proposing identities, belonging and customs that make economic and political governance possible by way of reinforcing the basic rules of civil society. In some respects, a large part of radical activism is induced by a significant part of the institutions. In a society that Colin Crouch calls 'post-democratic society', powerful minority interests have become far more active than the mass of ordinary people in making the political system work for them. Through top-down publicity campaigns, political elites have learned to manage and manipulate popular demands and persuade people to vote for a specific party. In many cases, an influential part of this class not only interprets and represents the will of this mass, it also sends signals which this mass then receives and reacts upon (Crouch, 2004).

In the following pages, I argue that institutions, especially welfare institutions, are becoming incapable of addressing the major social challenges of individualised society; that is to say, by enhancing welfare opportunities and a basic security net to deal with the requirements of an individualised existence. Social sustainability and the mutual compatibility of innovations and changes can be assessed on this basis, on shared principles and values, and a new guiding strategic framework.

4

The shifting relations with the welfare state

An uncertain distinction strategy

As discussed in Chapter 3, over the last two decades, there has been a growth, in many Western European countries, of an extended social stratum that, similar to Wilensky's 'middle mass' (1975; 2002), comprises a large part of the middle and working classes. This stratum is faced with particular processes of radical individualisation that have weakened ties between individuals and their social network and lowered trust in political institutions. In the last two decades, within a highly individualised and highly fragmented middle mass, widespread processes of economic deprivation and cultural backlash against progressive values have become increasingly relevant for their transformative power of social identities and consolidated living conditions. The OECD (2016; 2019) documents the pressures on the middle class in terms of its economic situation, living expenses, and labour market insecurity. At the EU level, more than half of middle–class people report a feeling of vulnerability and difficulty making ends meet. The proportion of the middle class which reports financial strain varies dramatically across European countries. While the Scandinavian and northern middle classes report very low levels of difficulty in making ends meet, others, mostly in central-eastern and southern European nations, are much more severely affected (European Commission, 2019: 53).

However, middle-class decline is an outcome not of single, isolated events but a combination of several risks and causal relationships: radical individualisation, weak individual and collective action, weak institutions and unstable informal relationships, market polarisation, low income and growing precarity, increased competition. In broad terms, the decline of the middle class emerges when the power transformation of some of these risks overwhelms the protective and inclusive relationships and resources existing within a context. In many cases, the issue is that highly individualised countries do not have institutional resources or networks of relations, values systems or individual reflexive modes to address many of the most significant social challenges and support positive social changes. Within this stratum, many authors (Hainsworth, 2000; Ignazi, 2003; Betz, 2004) have observed the rise of an 'extremism of the centre', a kind of individual activism and high level of electoral volatility which is harder to govern.

Welfare policies are currently growing less and less capable of managing these forms of individualism. New welfare configurations were introduced in the last two decades in order to confront new social risks and ensure the welfare state's long-term sustainability. To different degrees, strategies defined over the years as active welfare, new risk policies and social investment welfare have spread in all European countries and to many other countries worldwide. It was thought that an ageing demographic, changes in household structure and the negative effects of labour market dynamics were aspects of an irreversible transition to a post-industrial society. By identifying new social policy solutions and renewed strategies able to reconcile social and economic goals, Western societies could govern or smooth these changes. Many welfare programme recalibrations of the past two decades (Ferrera and Hemerijck, 2003; Bonoli, 2007; Emmenegger et al, 2012; Dwyer, 2017) have been promoted to confront the impact of demographic transitions and global competition on the sustainability of welfare, and the difficulties in reconciling work and family responsibilities (Farnsworth and Irving, 2015; Horfall and Hudson, 2017; Taylor-Gooby et al, 2017; Deeming and Smyth, 2018; Pierson, 2021).

Many authors have highlighted the prevalence of other social risks: the growing fragmentation and instability of social relations, the fragility of human bonds, the erosion of the main institutions and the need for welfare that ensures basic securities (Beck, 1992; Beck and Beck-Gernsheim 2001; Giddens, 1994b; Bauman, 2000). However, these analyses have contributed only in a limited way to rethinking welfare priorities, programmes and areas of intervention. The most significant reforms do not capture the policy implications of the anger and resentment felt by a large part of the people. The public debate emphasises the need for increased surveillance and punitive actions to face welfare dependency and the irregular behaviours of low-income families. The extension and intensification of welfare conditionality and other kinds of divisive welfare, such as welfare chauvinism, are the main responses for managing stigmatised and more problematic social groups and governing the poor and socially marginalised. This punitive perspective is not applied to the middle class; instead, retrenchment politics that make public welfare benefits and services less accessible for them are designed. These new welfare recalibrations are underestimating the extension and speed of the changes taking place in ordinary human relationships and are undermining the central institutions of contemporary society.

In many respects, a divided welfare state between the public and private spheres, conditional welfare and welfare chauvinism respond to the need for distinction that historically characterises the middle class. Particular ways of acting, speaking, thinking and 'individuating' are markers of 'class'. These are connected to a social position and constitute the historical track of its status position and the strategy for its conservation and the intergenerational transmission of an advantageous achievement in work, educational and social policies systems. As Bourdieu claimed (1984: 6), social subjects, classified by their classifications, distinguish themselves by the distinctions they make, between the beautiful and the ugly, the illustrious and the vulgar, in which their position in the objective classifications is expressed or betrayed.

Family socialisation passes on not only economic advantage or disadvantage, but also habitus, a complex schema of dispositions, taste and expectations (Bourdieu, 1977). In the last decade, a large segment of the middle class feels that uncertainty, economic deprivation, low upward mobility and cultural changes have made it increasingly difficult to adopt an individualised strategy aimed at distinguishing and reproducing the family's class habitus and their traditional social position, nullifying any stable sense of collective belonging and the support of informal relationships. Family socialisation processes are less effective in reproducing and emphasising class belonging, middle-class values and social identity.

The chapter is organised as follows. The first part gives a brief overview of the academic debate on the involvement of the middle class in the expansion of the welfare state. In the second and third parts, I seek to analyse how politics of retrenchment and new forms of dualisation are affecting the living conditions of the middle class. Some divisive configurations of welfare supported by substantial segments of the middle class are described in the following parts. At the end of the chapter, I argue that non-secondary segments of the middle class take on a different kind of radicalism. The middle class constitutes the primary social basis of many social welfare movements against discrimination and the exclusion of low-income families and minority ethnic groups. The chapter concludes with some further comments on the changing welfare attitudes of the middle class and on social divisions that are emerging between the higher and the lower middle class in defending the welfare state and social rights.

The middle class and the traditional welfare state

In the era of the great expansion of the welfare state (1960–1975), one of the most important aspects of its evolution was the nature of middle-class involvement. The expansion of the welfare state tended to confer disproportionate benefits on the middle classes and ensure this class a privileged position compared to less affluent social groups (Pierson, 1991: 129). These included access to higher quality of services and programmes in areas health, pensions, childcare and education. In the 1950s, responding to critics on the political 'right' who saw post-war welfare as expensive for the middle classes, Titmuss argued that it would be natural to assume that more welfare would mean more redistribution in favour of the poor. Instead, all the systems favour the middle and upper classes: higher income groups know how to make better use of services. Instead, the poor have great difficulties in managing change, choosing between alternatives, and finding their way around the complex world of welfare (Titmuss, 1958: 19). Social policies can no longer be thought of simply as a means of benefiting the poor at the expense of the rich (Titmuss, 1958). Titmuss (1958), identified three systems of welfare: social/public, fiscal and occupational. All three are manifestations of social policies that favour targeted groups in the population and provide similar benefits. The difference between the three sources of welfare is not functional, but only an organisational division of method. In fact, all three systems favour the middle classes and other groups, such as the upper classes, who know how to make better use of the services. Brian Abel-Smith in his essay 'Whose welfare state' (1958) highlights that middle-class people primarily benefited through free social services. The middle class gained more from the welfare state than the working class did and was the major beneficiary of welfare: it had better access to government social programmes and received better services than the working class.

Several years later, Le Grand (1982) also confirmed that welfare (especially in the health sector, education, old-age pensions) benefited the middle class more than the poor. Middle-class men and women, plus the immediate members of their families, had a significant interest in its preservation as both users and employees of important parts of the welfare state (Le Grand and Winter, 1986: 400). The impact of the service was far less egalitarian than was previously assumed, once proper account was taken of the capacity of higher-income groups to make use of health services, public education, housing programmes and transportation subsidies (Le Grand and Winter, 1986; Goodin and Le Grand, 1987). If groups compete for social benefits as for other goods, it is perhaps not surprising that the winners in the marketplace repeat the same results in the welfare domain (Baldwin, 1990: 26–27). On the other hand, the welfare state arises when influential middle-class sections see it as their interest to share risks with those less well-off than themselves. Overall, it can be safely argued that the middle class has played a key role in the development of the welfare state (Baldwin, 1990: 94).

More recent studies carried out in many countries suggest that better off groups still retain an advantage in relation to some services and that the redistributive capacity of the welfare state is diminishing (Duffy, 2000; Crozier et al, 2008; Hastings, 2009). The effects of redistributing social welfare transfers have had the same pro-poor pattern in all nations, but the middle quintiles are always a net beneficiary (Garfinkel et al, 2005). A review of the literature by Matthews and Hastings (2013) synthesised a wide range of academic research (65 empirical studies from the UK, the US and Scandinavian countries published between 1980 and 2012) examining whether, how and with what effect middle-class activism – distinguishing between collective and individual engagement – secures advantages for this group of service users. The research employed the realist synthesis approach

(Pawson, 2006) in reviewing existing research evidence. The review found that the middle class are in an advantaged position compared to less affluent social groups when it comes to accessing public services. Middle-class service users have the 'cultural capital' (education, networks, skills and resources) that helps them in negotiating with service providers, especially in the areas of schooling, health and neighbourhood planning. They also tend to share the same value set as bureaucrats – laying the basis for an alliance between middle-class service providers and users that works against the interests of the less affluent. Four causal theories were derived from this evidence, theories which explain advantage as the outcome of particular mechanisms operating in specific contexts. Two of the theories focused on the role of middle-class activism (the level or nature of the middle class as an interest group or on an individual basis). A third highlighted the importance of a cultural alignment between service providers and middle-class service users, while the fourth theory identified how middle-class needs and demands are 'normalised' in policy and delivery processes: these needs or expectations of quality of service are 'normalised' in both policy and practice, to the extent that policy priorities favour the middle classes (Matthews and Hastings, 2013: 14–15).

It is also possible that the belief that the middle class benefited disproportionally from the welfare state has been exaggerated (Powell, 1995). However, some advantages gained in the past have clearly diminished in recent years. The emerging welfare configurations respond less and less to the needs of substantial middle-class segments. The welfare state is an arena that generates 'the Matthew effect' (Merton, 1968): initial advantage tends to beget further advantage, and disadvantage further disadvantage, creating widening gaps between people with limited personal resources and people with more (Rigney, 2010: 1).

Welfare becomes a sphere of life in which many governments and political parties try to reconstruct the distinctions of the middle class and working class compared to other social groups, establishing and legitimising the differences, recreating those distinct identities between different social groups. For many reasons, a large part of the middle class feels the need to follow this distinction strategy, being afraid of a further worsening in terms of income, style of life, quality of work, stability, and access to social and health services.

A series of declines in economic and political terms for the middle class change its relation to welfare, its chances to access welfare services and its influence on many transformations processes and political reforms.

The collective revolts of the middle mass

In the middle of the 1970s, Wilensky observed the revolt of the more dynamic segment of the middle mass against welfare in the US and, with very similar characteristics, in nearly all European countries. The taxpayers' revolt emerged, in particular, where the middle mass perceived its tax burden to be unfair relative to that of the rich and the upper middle class and felt increasing social distance from the poor, while private welfare was becoming increasingly limited (Wilensky, 1975: 68; 1976). In those years, social and political subjects in many European countries encountered difficulty developing a feasible programme for the defence and development of the welfare state. It had to meet three conditions: provisions needed to be generous and inclusive and have collective support; it had to be seen as feasible; and it had to be effective in delivering the desired outcome (Taylor-Gooby, 2013: 49).

In the following decades, this trilemma would go on to mark the evolution of the welfare state in a distinct manner. In the 1980s and in the 1990s, popular support for welfare steadily declined in many Western countries, weakening parties that had traditionally supported it and creating new social divisions within the middle mass. A large part of public opinion changed, moving from a support for collective solutions to problems of social needs to a preference for market provision to satisfy individual welfare demands (Taylor-Gooby, 1985; Pierson, 1991: 150). The welfare state was not simply considered a victim of poor economic performance but one of its principal causes (Pierson, 1994: 4). Economic stagnation, technological changes, high unemployment and growing labour market insecurity created much tax resistance. A large portion of the middle mass is involved in collective protest against some expensive welfare programmes, the soaring tax burden, and the universalistic principle that ensured benefits to the entire population without consideration of their ability to pay (Rothstein, 1998).

> When lower-white collar workers and upper-blue-collar workers look up, they see an overprivileged, college-educated upper middle class and the rich, who seem to evade taxes, live well, indulge their children who run wild at expensive colleges or worse, at state universities, at their expense. When they look down, they see the welfare poor and immigrants whose moral lifestyle, and ethnic-racial origin repel them, whose children, they think, are at the root of crime and disorder. These citizens of the middle mass see themselves as working hard at disciplined jobs, living by rules, struggling for a decent, safe home and more job security, fighting against the erosion of their earning and standard of living. (Wilensky, 2002: 394)

From the 1990s onward, many European nations, such as the Netherlands, France, Germany and Italy, have put pressure on introducing more selectivity in granting benefits and reducing all levels of benefits. A large part of the middle class 'feels the tax squeeze' and considered benefits for the poor too generous (income support, free education, housing benefits) and increasingly being paid by people like them. It is assumed that many claimants do not deserve the benefits they receive and do not do everything they can to find work.

Much research observes the evolution of all three systems of welfare (social/public, fiscal and occupational) identified by Titmuss, and shows that in the last decades low-income households have seen their welfare benefits progressively reduced. However, cuts in social spending have also affected a large part of the middle class in similar ways (Garfinkel et al, 2005; Smeeding, 2005; Pressman, 2007).

Taken together, economic, political and social changes were clear signals of a deep structural crisis of industrial society and a long-lasting transition towards a highly individualised society. In all European countries, processes of individualisation eroded traditional structures such as the extended family and religious groups, while at the same time creating new structures (national trade unions, political parties, large hierarchical firms and associations). In the last two decades, a radical individualisation freed the individual from both old and new forms of social belonging.

The coalition between the working class and the middle class which underlies the major expansion of welfare started to loosen, leaving room for a multitude of other coalitions. There is ample evidence that in countries where means testing dominates, a segment of the middle class has allied itself with the upper class to contain welfare spending, from which it receives little benefits. Where universalism prevails, the middle class has formed coalitions with the working class to alter the market distribution of resources, by redistributing incomes from the upper income class to themselves (Gugushvili and Laenen, 2019: 9).

In the 1990s, Paul Pierson noted in an influential book that retrenchment occurred when supporting interest groups were weak or when the government found ways to prevent the mobilisation of these groups' supporters (1994: 6). Retrenchment, by his definition, is a policy change that both cuts social expenditure and restructures social programmes towards a more residual welfare state model (p 17). Pierson argued that the results of retrenchment efforts had varied significantly within and across policy arenas and distinct programmes even though they were limited overall. Social policy is the most resilient component of the post-war order (1994: 5–6). Le Grand and Winter (1986) showed that those services most used by the middle classes were protected from expenditure cuts implemented as part of its austerity programme. The middle class uses its considerable political skills to obtain more resources or to defend them in periods of decline (Goodin and Le Grand, 1987: 210). Esping-Andersen (1990: 33) comes to a similar conclusion, stating that social democratic and corporatist welfare-state regimes that tend to be universalistic and were founded by a class coalition would be less likely to suffer from the politics of welfare retrenchment.

In actual fact, the resilience of the welfare state is more apparent than real, as documented by a large body of theoretical and empirical research. Changes in policy purpose have occurred even in cases where formal policy structure has been relatively stable (Hacker, 2004: 70). The real limit of Pierson's and others' analyses is the emphasis on active legislative reform, excluding from consideration 'hidden types of change' that are less visible means of erosion of the welfare state (Hacker, 2004: 245; Starke, 2008).

Many 'hidden types of change' have eroded European welfare states: budgetary measures that progressively reduce resources in the health system and in old-age pensions; the introduction of new selective policies without eliminating old programmes; apparently secondary governmental decisions that have made a programme of income support more selective. In fact, in many European countries, the distinction between different forms of retrenchment, from active legislative reforms to 'hidden types of change', has revealed itself decisive in minimising the political resistance of significant parts of the working and the middle class. While organic proposals for the reform of old-age pensions or the health systems have contributed to remarkable protests of the middle and working classes, 'hidden changes' have led to a mobilisation of just small segments of these classes.

Different kinds of politics of retrenchment are being largely implemented in many European countries, though to a lesser extent in many countries of Continental Europe such as France and Germany, where interest organisations have contained cutbacks and recalibrations. Deep economic crises or the need to reduce budget deficits and restore economic growth and employment by withdrawing benefits from 'undeserving groups' have become the principal circumstances that justify the politics of welfare retrenchment (Levy, 1999; 2012).

Austerity and retrenchment are some of the terms used extensively in the public debate and in the academic literature on the development of welfare states. They were first used mainly in the context of the consequences of the economic crisis in the 1970s, like stagnation and inflation, and continued during the recent financial crises from 2009 onwards (Greve, 2020). Over the last two decades, compared to previous versions, a more radical form of retrenchment is emerging based on its assimilation into neoliberal thought. Austerity and retrenchment go beyond simple cuts in public spending to reconfiguring and transforming welfare states more deeply and undermining all welfare institutions and structures and the groups and the social relations they support (Farnsworth and Irving, 2015: 13–15). Austerity is a dangerous idea because it ignores the externalities it generates and the impact of one person's choices on another's (Blyth, 2015: 14). The COVID-19 pandemic is likely reversing these social and institutional trends that seemed relentless;

a renewed emphasis on the need to strengthen the role of the state is hindering every strategy towards progressive privatisation of welfare and the enhancement of the politics of retrenchment.

The changing trajectory of middle-class positions

A considerable amount of research shows a progressive middle-class shift in welfare support and changes in the welfare class coalition from the traditional middle-and-working-class alliance to a 'middle class–business' one (Gingrich and Häusermann, 2015; Häusermann and Palier, 2017). In many aspects, the politics of retrenchment might be seen as a response to political pressure from a cross-class coalition of employers and workers in multinational sectors (Clayton and Pontusson, 1998). The main point of contention in welfare politics is no longer simply the size of the welfare state but also what the welfare state should do: invest in human skills or substitute income. Voters on the radical right take a clear stance in favour of consumption policies that include measures such as old-age pensions or unemployment benefits. The primary aim is to compensate for income losses while opposing social investment policies (Enggist and Pingerra, 2021).

Over the past two to three decades, a strong social division has emerged between the more dynamic segment of the middle class and the 'new middle mass' regarding three main aspects of welfare policies: cuts to social spending; social investment policies; and support for configurations of divisive welfare. A large number of studies have documented that the more educated segment that enjoys a higher socioeconomic status has two main welfare attitudes. A large segment tends to support social investment programmes on capital formation and early childcare education and also believes that conventional income maintenance guarantees must be scaled down. However, there are high middle-class segments that are explicitly anti-welfare and arguing for a drastic reduction of the role of the state, mainly due to the unsustainable rise of the tax burden and what this implies (Gingrich and Häusermann, 2015; Häusermann and Palier, 2017; Fenger, 2018).

A large part of the middle mass is less satisfied with welfare state outcomes and the quality of public institutions (European Social Survey, 2018). However, they support and defend the welfare state and request better protection of the 'losers' of globalisation. These people believe that selective cuts to social spending and some politics of retrenchment are necessary, reasonable and fair, as some recipients do not deserve welfare benefits and migrants and asylum seekers make excessive use of welfare. Sometimes, they approve of imposing forms of conditionality and strict welfare chauvinism in more radical terms.

Many of these people want a particularistic-authoritarian welfare state, displaying moderate support only for 'deserving' benefit recipients (for example, the elderly), while revealing strong support for a workfare approach and little support for social investment (Busemeyer et al, 2021). However, granting rights based on reciprocity (having paid taxes for a reasonable period) is the most popular position by far (Taylor-Gooby et al, 2017; European Social Survey, 2018; Fenger, 2018), combined with a feeling of nostalgia for the lost 'golden age' or 'good old days' of the welfare state, when assistance was generous for those who worked hard and the deserving poor and needy (2021: 1).

The public and academic debate on the middle classes and their relationship to welfare, which is ongoing in all European countries, is clearly illustrated by Barbehön, Geugjes and Haus' research (Barbehön and Haus, 2015; Barbehön et al, 2020). In summing up the current public, political and academic debates in Germany, these authors identify three distinct narratives, all of them characterised by a specific framing of the middle class and its relation to the welfare state.

A first narrative is organised around the notion of a plundered middle. Here the middle class is portrayed as the efficient and motivated core of society in contrast to both the poor and the rich. Social policies that are perceived to run against middle-class interests are portrayed as a kind of expropriation. The middle class is constantly under threat of exploitation by passive, envious and dependent underclass members, on the one hand, and greedy capital owners, on the other hand. The second narrative asserts a manifest crisis of the middle class, but one that results from the growing risks stemming from large-scale systemic powers like globalisation, neoliberalism or New Public Management. By referring to the threat of precarity and exclusion, this narrative constructs the middle not as the stable core but as a fragile and vulnerable realm. The welfare state is blamed for no longer providing protection against the increasing risks of modern society. Finally, a third narrative clearly differs from the other two in that it de-dramatises the widespread alerts that identify serious middle-class crises. Instead, it is claimed that the middle class is in a privileged position or even benefiting from economic and political changes. This beneficial position is secured at the expense of both the upper and the lower classes and future generations.

Individualising welfare solutions

The last three decades have seen the welfare state reconfigured in many key sectors and programmes, through increasing state control over public welfare expenditure and new combinations of providers, progressive privatisation (Farnsworth and Irving, 2015; Siza, 2019), a rewriting of social contracts in order to de-emphasise social rights and place a stronger emphasis on individual responsibilities (Horsfall and Hudson, 2017: 3), more stringent targets, and cut backs of the provision for the poor, migrants and the non-working population (Taylor-Gooby et al, 2017: 9).

Reforms and recalibrations have been organised with the aim of undermining traditional redistributive functions and the traditional welfare regimes towards hybrid welfare models that combine, in terms deemed financially sustainable, features of liberal welfare systems with those of social democratic ones, weakening public sectors through conservative-corporate models. The emphasis has shifted from protecting people from the market, extending transfers of welfare provisions and redistributive policies to empowering individuals to compete more successfully in the market (Schmidtke, 2002: 12).

In countries like France, Germany and the Netherlands, the quality of public provision and traditional levels of benefits have changed. The middle class remains the most significant beneficiary of welfare, but it is encouraged to opt into a private welfare market, usually through tax incentives (Schmidtke, 2002: 12; Humpage, 2015). It can easily improve its situation more in market investments than in collective forms of solidarity, which are increasingly viewed as fragile (Mau, 2015: 101). In the UK, in the first decade of the new millennium, the New Labour government embraced the managerialism of its predecessors, attempting to balance responsibility with rights and identifying a wide range of a welfare subject's agency: citizen-consumers acting in the pursuit of enlightened self-interested; the vulnerable who needed support; and welfare dependants who needed to exercise their responsibilities to be off welfare and in paid work. Another subject's agency emerged from new social movements, community-based groups and organisations, emphasising the importance of voice, empowerment and control in access to welfare provisions (Williams, 2021: 123).

In all European countries, rights and welfare services are individualised to respond to individualised families. For example, addiction and disabilities are individual problems rather than relational ones that can be faced through individualised solutions without considering interactions and interdependencies or involving the relationships with other family members and reorganising the entire family patterns. Activation strategies shift away from the family, its resources, ties and critical relations; active citizens are expected to organise their support and care resources individually.

As stated by Valkenburg (2007) and later by Borghi and van Berkel (2007: 414–415) in the context of social policies, we may identify five different discourses on individualised welfare solutions. The first discourse, individualising social services, is conceived as a necessary response to the increased differentiation and flexibility of social, cultural and economic life. The second discourse coincides largely with the idea of transferring resources from public welfare institutions to the private hands of welfare clients, enabling the latter to decide for themselves what services or goods they need to overcome their difficulties. A third corresponds to a general shift of responsibilities from the public sphere to the private sphere (the realm of individuals and their families). A fourth conceives it as an answer to the increasing erosion of the family as an economic unit, whereby the increasing individualisation of life-courses are often interpreted as pressures towards social policies that address individuals, independently of their position in the family structure. A final perspective insists on the increasing reflexivity of individual and social life: instead of offering predefined and standardised solutions to their problems, social policies and institutions should empower and promote policy users' reflexivity regarding their life projects.

In many ways, I believe that these five discourses respond to the needs of an individualised middle class that autonomously builds the set of welfare services it needs by putting together public and private services. The active citizen is nothing but a welfare consumer, responsible for their own choices, flexible and highly mobile, who seeks non-standard solutions, who is able to purchase a wider range of services directly from competitive public and private welfare providers without constraints and collective commitments. This is an active citizen's social identity that finally has reduced the burden and moral ties with those reliant on the welfare state.

Individualised welfare is tailored to a modern, active and dynamic individualised family – which would certainly not consider using exclusively public services to meet its main requirements in the healthcare system, education and long-term care. The commonly shared belief is that a considerable part of this class is dynamic, active and able to invest a portion of its income to ensure effective and high-quality private services that provide protection against the risks of life such as ageing, illness or job loss.

In reality, middle-class conditions are extremely varied. The term middle class refers to a broad swathe of the population, encompassing a wide variety of occupational groupings consisting both of people who occupy social positions that provide them with material and cultural advantages and people whose income is low and status precarious (Hacker, 2013; Parker, 2013). The welfare reforms promoted in many European countries (especially the Netherlands, Germany and France) increased the social division between more dynamic segments of the middle class (more educated and with higher socioeconomic status) and the lower middle class. For many reasons, the former was the main culturally and politically active subject, and the latter the primary victim. These reforms have met the needs of identity and distinction of the middle classes as a whole, yet have also significantly contributed to a worsening of the economic conditions of the lower segments.

Welfare is recreating distinctions and those diverging identities between social groups that the labour market has blurred. In the last two decades, welfare has become a sphere of life in which many governments and social and political actors recognise and legitimise the distinctions between the lower and upper middle class, compared to other social groups, and places a strong emphasis on nationalist values, establishing conditionality and legitimising differences in relation to low-income households. A large part of the new middle mass, in turn, feels the need to create new distinctions in the welfare arena, searching for personal achievement with lower taxes and without collective rules and constraints. It is afraid of losing its identity and seeing a further worsening of its position in terms of income, style of life, quality of work, stability, and access to social and health services. It defends middle-class social identity by aggressively refusing to share the culture, lifestyle and network of relations of low-income households.

An activism that does not work

European governments cannot ignore the middle class's individual and collective radical activism aimed both at reaffirming a social identity (an intentional choice in their access to welfare), cutting benefits, and being stricter in distributing provisions for migrants and the undeserving poor. Mau states (2015: ix) that in democratic societies, it is entirely improbable that a political project catches on without garnering the support of political majorities.

In many Western societies governing alliances have emerged in recent years that Hacker and Pierson (2020: 6–12) called 'plutocratic populism'. Conservative parties in a democratic society cannot win elections by only protecting economic elites. They must expand that base, which means persuading working- and middle-class voters to focus not on their financial self-interest, but on race, conservative religious values and other perceived identity threats while making some concessions such as allowing some policies that benefit these groups.

Though overall outcomes are not positive for the fragmented middle class, they do not change government policy. The reforms and the recalibrations of the programmes and instruments that have been created (politics of retrenchment, politics of austerity, new forms of dualisation, chauvinism and conditional welfare) are not updated. However, these welfare reforms have not been proven capable of overcoming the decline and addressing the worsening of the living conditions of a large part of the middle class. Over the last three decades, a large part of this class has lost a variety of certainties relating to work stability and income, and is exposed to similar uncertainties in other spheres of life, such as welfare, family and informal relations. Only a small section of the middle class has improved their condition, while the vast majority of families have lost job security, their income has been eroded, and their prospects of upward mobility have decreased (Pressman, 2007; Atkinson, 2015; Parker, 2013). A large majority struggle to live their own lives in a world that increasingly escapes their grasp (Beck and Beck-Gernsheim, 2001: 25).

All the core aspects of middle-class life have been weakened: a job with reasonable pay; the ability to raise a family without undue hardship; basic economic security grounded in homeownership; and the opportunity to rise up the economic ladder through education and hard work (Hacker, 2010).

An influential OECD report from 2019 indicates that the middle income class has experienced dismal income growth or even stagnation over the past three decades in all European countries. Achieving a middle-class lifestyle has also become more difficult than in the past. A middle-class lifestyle is typically associated with certain goods and services and certain living conditions, such as decent housing, good education and good and accessible health services. However, the prices of core consumption goods and services such as health, education and housing have risen well above inflation, while middle incomes have been lagging behind (OECD, 2019).

Hacker argued (2013: 145) that globalisation and technological change do matter, but their effects have been heavily shaped by whether and how governments have responded to them. Market dynamics are not 'natural' but are constituted by government policy and political institutions (Hacker and Pierson, 2010). Thus, political decisions and choices play a key role in the decline of the middle class. In many Western societies, institutional responses, especially of political institutions and welfare systems, have been weak or misjudged. Making government more responsive to the needs and concerns of the middle class would not be just a political achievement; it would mean having to reshape the economy (Hacker, 2013). Of course, changing the political landscape and making these choices is not easy; introducing marked distinctions between classes and selective welfare for the less deserving groups is undoubtedly politically easier. Dualisation, conditionality and chauvinism constitute key dimensions of the new welfare proposed by governments and parties that a large part of the middle classes has not opposed, responding to a new desired social identity founded on radical self-reliance.

Stabilising social divisions: the divided welfare state

In the US, Hacker (2002) documents and analyses the divided public and private social benefits system. Social spending is as high as that in many European nations. What is truly distinctive is 'the prominent place of tax expenditures in providing and subsidising private social benefits' (p 294). This system tends to become less able to redistribute income and risks down the income ladder. Privatised social welfare approaches 'depoliticise' policy by moving it outside of routine political channels and into the realm of market relations, when it is governed not by collective political decisions, but by negotiations between individual workers and employers (p 44). A divided welfare state is consolidated when the private and less visible sector erodes public welfare by encouraging self-reliance and free enterprise for new actors, all of which are interested in continued welfare privatisation (Hacker, 2002: 18; Palier, 2012: 252).

Referring to the European countries, Lapidus (2019) argued that within the same nation, there are two very different welfare states: one is the welfare state aimed at some low-income groups and the other is hidden welfare (such as private health insurance, private education system) that primarily benefits people in the higher income strata and excludes large part of the population. The hidden welfare state grows at the expense of the universal welfare state, which everyone has traditionally used (Lapidus, 2019).

Historically, dualisation has characterised two realms of welfare: job protection and pensions. In terms of job protection, a key determining factor of dualisation have been the different occupational profiles of workers and a distinction between 'insiders' and 'outsiders'. Insiders are groups with highly protected jobs who do not feel greatly threatened by high levels of unemployment. On the other hand, outsiders are either unemployed or hold jobs characterised by low salaries and low levels of social protection, employment rights, benefits and social security privileges (Rueda, 2005: 62; Rubery, 2007). Two side-effects of these changes to the welfare system have been the division of the population between insured insiders and assisted or activated outsiders (Palier, 2010) and the growing forms of dualisation in terms of access to benefits, efficiency and quality of services (Palier and Kathleen, 2010; Seeleib-Kaiser et al, 2011). Dualisation is described by Emmenegger et al (2012: 10) as a 'differentiation of rights, entitlement and services provided to different categories of recipient'. It may take on three different forms: a deepening of existing institutional dualism, that is, the differential treatment of insiders and outsiders becoming more pronounced; a widening of existing institutional dualisms, namely, groups that have been previously treated as insiders are increasingly treated as outsiders; or finally, it may be the product of a new institutional dualism as a result of non-intervention in the face of external pressure (Emmenegger et al, 2012: 10–11).

In a 'hybrid welfare' system and after many years of austerity and politics of retrenchment, new forms of dualisation are emerging that are not solely based on the distinction between the 'insiders' and 'outsiders' of the labour market and employment rights. New forms of dualisation affect the large majority of people and their chances of both access to public and private welfare and the efficiency and quality of services they use. Especially in the health and public education systems, the protection offered by public services is no longer sufficient. The population is increasingly divided between those who enjoy adequate private protection, and those (low middle class and working class) who are covered by very limited private services and occupational schemes. Public services are increasingly incapable of creating opportunities for these individuals through active support programmes. In Nordic welfare states, as in the south European welfare states, although public services contribute less and less to the improvement of the living conditions of this social stratum, private welfare provision plays a compensatory role almost exclusively for social groups with consolidated incomes and employment. This welfare evolution places the central classes of the social stratification at risk of not enjoying sufficient public services and having only a limited ability to access private insurance. Private welfare in the health sector and education is mainly available to the established middle class. The word universal welfare state takes on a completely different meaning. It does not refer to a collective social right that rests on universalism, solidarity and 'decommodification', but to a means-tested welfare service directed at the most vulnerable groups (Lapidus, 2019).

Many years ago, Titmuss (1958) argued that occupational welfare relates to the employed population and benefits are thus related to achievement. This situation remains unchanged. Occupational welfare tends to favour those already embedded in the labour market and to exclude those who are not employed, have a precarious employment situation or work in small companies that do not provide their employees with welfare benefits. Furthermore, many workers are poorly paid and lack economic security while simultaneously experiencing working conditions difficult to reconcile with family life, even in the presence of welfare support programmes.

Regulating the conduct of low-income populations

Despite the fact that the middle class requires the state and is consequently oriented towards protecting its rights, it also pursues interests that can stand in opposition to a well-funded security state (Mau, 2015: 101–102). Recent years have seen neoliberalism lose much of its appeal among the middle class as a policy model and ideology emphasising the value of free-market competition. Instead, what remains is a neoliberal way of thinking about every aspect of ordinary life, evaluating choices and activities, actions and behaviours of people who live in poverty and do not lead an independent life, and several inclusive aspects of welfare policies. Individuals who are builders of their biographies become the norm against which other logics of action are judged. Neoliberalism still shapes every process of individualisation, emphasising its instrumental dimensions.

The neoliberal and anti-welfare positions have gradually been transformed into support for more selective welfare for migrants and 'undeserving' people. The European Social Survey shows that Europeans share a common and fundamental culture of deservingness: across countries and social categories, there is a consistent pattern that elderly people are seen as most deserving, closely followed by people with disabilities, the unemployed are seen as less deserving still, and immigrants as the least deserving of all. What a significant part of the middle class seems to solicit from parties and governments is 'welfare protectionism' that shields the privileges of old beneficiaries against the claims, needs and demands of new risk groups and stands at the expense of growing groups of outsiders who have no access to decent social protection (Häusermann, 2012). However, research also shows that protests today tend to overrepresent the middle classes and underrepresent low-income groups, and that the former are more politically active than the latter (Della Porta, 2015; Trenz and Grasso, 2018; Giugni and Grasso, 2019: 200).

All European governments are introducing several measures based on harsh conditionality. In Denmark, the traditional universal and inclusive welfare regime that provides equal services to all citizens, independently of their individual contributions, has undergone an important, and often unnoticed, transformation over the last decade. Through a series of reforms, provision has generally become more conditional and distinctions between various layers of need have been introduced (Trenz and Grasso, 2018). A similar evolution is notable in the welfare systems of France, the United Kingdom, the Netherlands and Italy. Most people tend to be more supportive of these conditional welfare schemes when they are targeted at groups they perceive as more undeserving (van Oorschot, 2006). This is in contrast to groups perceived to be more deserving, such as those who have contributed to their nation before (who have earned their support), or who may be expected to be able to contribute in the future (van Oorschot, 2000).

Welfare conditionality requires people to behave in a certain way to access welfare goods, such as cash benefits, housing or support services. Conditional arrangements combine elements of sanction, financial penalties and support to change welfare recipients' behaviour and regulate the conduct of low-income populations (Watts et al, 2014; Dwyer, 2019). Clasen and Clegg (2007: 172–174) identify three types of conditions that can be established in order for a person to receive social security. The first condition is that of being a member of a defined category of support (unemployed, disabled, homeless). The second condition is eligibility and entitlement criteria (passing means tests, having a particular level of need). The third type pertains to behavioural requirements and constraints imposed upon different kinds of benefit recipients. Since the mid-1980s, all Western European countries have applied the first two conditions; in the last decade, they have also added the third condition, progressively increasing controls and exclusions. In UK the punitive turn began in 2010, with the application of tightened sanctions requirements as well as an increase of the duration and severity of sanctions for failing to meet these requirements (Immervoll and Knotz, 2018).

What has been central to the shift is the requirement that certain groups who had previously enjoyed access to largely unconditional benefits have now become responsible, active agents in their own welfare (Dwyer, 2017: 135). Despite the policy rhetoric of autonomy, empowerment and enablement, these capacity-building initiatives are portrayed as attempts to discipline welfare recipients through close surveillance and the imposition of narrow neoliberal identities and subjectivities (Brady, 2007).

Conditionality is now applied to previously exempt groups such as lone parents and people with disabilities (Langenbucher, 2015) and in a broadening range of welfare spheres (Watts and Fitzpatrick, 2018). Groups who have been disproportionately affected by intensifying welfare conditionality are the unemployed, minority ethnic groups, young people, people with disabilities, low-income families with children, social tenants and the homeless. While governments seem relatively comfortable in supporting the powerful and nudging the middle class, they show persistent tendencies to direct harsher treatment at the poor or the disadvantaged (Harrison and Sanders, 2014: 11). Welfare conditionality is seen as an attempt to curb the irresponsible behaviour of a problematic population (Flint, 2006).

In conditional welfare, the focus is increasingly placed on individual responsibility and labour market participation, restricting the rights of social beneficiaries (Cantillon and Vandenbroucke, 2014). In this configuration of welfare, social citizenship becomes a disciplinary tool in promoting and regulating people's behaviour (Lister, 2011; Watts and Fitzpatrick, 2018). This new conceptualisation of social citizenship emphasises the validity of paid employment as central to its definition and as a primary citizenship obligation, undermining the value and legitimacy of informal care, the activities of parenting and other social obligations located in both the private domestic sphere and the public one (Isin, 2008; Lister, 2011). It is not that social rights are being extinguished; rather, they are being configured in ways more akin to property rights (Dean, 2015: 13) and have been marginalised by an increasing conditionality to the provision of social services and the ascendancy of a highly liberal-individualist conception of rights (Dean, 2020b: 7). Reframing social citizenship around a logic of individualised responsibility 're-commodifies the social rights of the majority' (Dwyer, 2016; 2017).

> If conditions among the lower classes deteriorated, it was because they failed for personal and cultural reasons to enhance their own human capital through education, the acquisition of a protestant work ethic, and submission to work discipline and flexibility. In short, problems arose because of the lack of competitive strength or because of personal, cultural, and political failing. (Harvey, 2007: 34)

The data linking conditional welfare to three policy outcomes – labour market inclusion, poverty reduction and positive behavioural change – are quite weak (Watts et al, 2014; Watts and Fitzpatrick, 2018: 93). Sanctions for employment-related conditions strongly reduce benefit use and increase people exiting from benefits, with generally unfavourable effects on longer-term outcomes (Griggs and Evans, 2010: 5).

Stabilising social distance: support for welfare chauvinism

From the 1990s onwards, working- and middle-class concern for supporting and defending the traditional welfare system has been changing. Popular support for traditional redistributive policies has declined, and support for different welfare configurations is on the rise. A considerable part of these social strata adheres to anti-immigration stances and express dissatisfaction with mainstream parties and central institutions. They also put increasing pressure towards a new configuration of welfare that restricts access to benefits or lowers the level of benefits for immigrants, ethnic minorities and traditionally undeserving groups. A combination of nativism, authoritarianism and populism are the core of its ideology (Mudde, 2007: 26).

The petite bourgeois and the losers of modernisation, particularly young, less-educated blue-collar workers, may be driven by welfare that encourages their rejection of foreigners in order to preserve the social safety net for native citizens (Kitschelt and McGann, 1997: 259). People who experience less income security feel more threatened by immigrants and are thus more chauvinistic. People who feel more economically secure are less threatened by immigrants and are therefore less supportive of welfare chauvinism (Mathijs and Coenders, 2019).

Andersen and Bjørklund (1990: 212) thought that 'welfare state chauvinism' – the conviction that welfare services should be restricted to 'our own' – is the most appropriate definition for this configuration of welfare. The term, however, has not been used consistently to denote the same welfare configuration. In many cases, it implies a welfare configuration which tries to reinforce the social protection of 'native globalisation losers' by increasing benefits, placing less emphasis on individual responsibility, and reducing competition with ethnic minorities on access to health, housing programmes and social assistance. In others, 'welfare chauvinism' is in favour of the 'victims of retrenchment policies' implemented by establishment parties at the expense of the 'native' population and to the benefit of the 'undeserving' immigrants and those people whose values and behaviour are considered the primary cause of their condition.

Welfare chauvinism is a typical populist response to establishment parties that were involved in downsizing the welfare state. Populist parties embrace a pro-welfare stance in an attempt to pit the people (victims of retrenchment) against the elite (those who attack the established welfare rights of the people); blaming both the elites for cutting the welfare rights of deserving 'natives' and the non-natives for their excessive claims on the welfare state (Schumacher and van Kersbergen, 2016). The political discussion on who deserves and who does not deserve the benefits and services becomes a central issue of populist proposals to change welfare (Greve, 2019).

Previous influential research (Betz, 1994) argued that populist parties advocated for individual achievement, a free market and a drastic reduction of the role of the state. In the last two decades, these parties have increasingly taken on a welfare chauvinistic position and criticise mainstream parties for cutting welfare for 'native' populations and benefiting 'undeserving' immigrants (Schumacher and van Kersbergen, 2016). Mainstream parties betrayed their working- and middle-class base by choosing immigration and European integration over the material and spiritual welfare of the people, thus letting down pensioners, the ill, the unemployed and other needy natives (2021: 10).

On a demand-side perspective, we can observe that support for welfare chauvinism is increasing among the middle mass. Many fear that migrants, refugees and the undeserving poor 'put additional burdens on a competitive society' and can weaken the relative security that welfare ensures.

Following the age of dualisation: towards a 'third welfare system'?

During the 1970s in the United States, Dale Tussing (1974) highlighted the simultaneous existence of two welfare systems.

> One is well known. It is explicit, poorly funded, stigmatised and stigmatising, and is directed at the poor. The other, practically unknown, is implicit, literally invisible, is non-stigmatised and non-stigmatising, and provides vast but unacknowledged benefits to the non-poor – whether working class, middle class or well to do. ... 'Social insurance', the heart of the welfare system for the non-poor, has been constructed to be legitimate, to protect the integrity and dignity of the people involved. ... 'Public charity', or the welfare system for the poor, has been constructed to be illegitimate. ... The illegitimacy of poor people's welfare is multifold. There is, first, the illegitimacy of dependency – living off the incomes of others. (Tussing, 1974: 50)

In the same period in Europe, the oil crisis, low economic growth rates, a legitimation crisis and taxpayers' revolts increased the pressure for cutting expensive public programmes and involving the resources of other sectors (market, third sector and informal sphere) in the production and delivery of welfare. Charities, voluntary organisations, self-help and community groups were beginning to be an integral part of a mixed economy of welfare. These non-state and non-market organisations operated in partnership with the state and private sector to provide welfare services for children, older people, and in health and social care.

Since the beginning of the 21st century, the traditional commitment of European countries to inclusive welfare and a mixed welfare system has considerably weakened. A fragmented system of welfare has emerged, allowing for deep social divisions in terms of access to benefits, efficiency and quality of services guaranteed to different middle-class segments and to middle-class and low-income households. Charities and community initiatives play a new role, in many cases no longer in partnership with professional services but working alone to support marginalised groups excluded from the formal welfare system.

Following the age of dualisation highlighted by Emmenegger et al (2012), a 'third welfare system' has been becoming stronger in many parts of Europe. It is welfare for some groups of the 'precariat', mainly ethnic minorities and asylum seekers.

A large number of welfare sectors have been paying growing attention to race, ethnicity and beneficiary behaviour, introducing severe conditional measures and multiple discrimination in access to benefits. Welfare conditionality and welfare chauvinism have led to an increase in the size of the 'disconnected' population receiving neither welfare payments nor work earnings (Watts and Fitzpatrick, 2018: 93). The end result is a decrease of public welfare claimants. Only a part of this population improves its social conditions, while a large part detaches from welfare services and turns to the 'third welfare system' provided by many charities and local public institutions, which distribute basic goods for day-to-day living and ensure temporary economic support. Benefit sanctions and the implementation of the workfare paradigm have been identified as key factors driving demand for food banks in European countries such as the United Kingdom, Germany and France (Lambie-Mumford and Silvasti, 2021).

The 'third welfare system' is welfare for a portion of the old and new 'underclass' and those social groups that Sassen (2014) defined as the people 'expelled' from the core social and economic order of our time, from welfare as well as from corporate insurance and unemployment support; in short, from the world of human rights. In Sassen's approach, expelled people are distinguished from the more common poor population. The latter exists inside a system and, in that sense, can be reduced. The former is only managed by increasing surveillance and minimal support measures and often without hope for the social integration of these most deprived and undeserving populations. People expelled do not become invisible. Deemed dangerous communities that constantly threaten our towns' safety, they are targeted for increased surveillance and the early identification of crime.

Middle-class support for an inclusive welfare

However, as we will see in the next chapter, new collaborative relationships, new opportunities for social dialogue and alternative ways of looking at the world are also emerging within the middle class. Significant middle-class segments promote active social initiatives capable of strengthening civic values and trust in other people and rebuilding a sense of belonging and identity. These are important segments of the middle class that tend to support social investment programmes and believe in inclusive welfare that generates and promotes well-being within the family, strengthens community relationships and is able to create neighbourhood communities more sensitive to the common good.

The middle class constitutes the main social basis of many contemporary movements fighting for social justice for refugees and migrant workers, aimed at preventing and solving poverty and child poverty, against the discrimination of people with disabilities and mental health service users. New social movements reflect the post-material values of the new middle classes (Fominaya and Cox, 2014; G. Martin, 2015: 64) and seem to express what Bourdieu (1987) called the cultural capital of the middle class (Annetts et al, 2009). More highly educated middle-class groups become engaged in demonstrations on cultural issues linked to matters regarding education, health services, childcare and other public services (Giugni and Grasso, 2019: 69).

New welfare movements operate in and around an already established welfare state system. They share several main features: preserving, extending and improving service delivery, resisting reductions or 'cuts' in services and defending the very principle of social welfare. The current welfare system has been subject to a radical critique and redefinition by these movements (Annetts et al, 2009: 10–11; Williams, 2021). In new ways, these movements have expressed similar values and raised awareness of wider issues such as the environment (Grasso and Giugni, 2022), gender, sexuality and ethnicity.

New social movements are born as collective action focused or organised around the consumption and/or control of important services and/or the meeting of individual, household or group needs and aspirations, outside the sphere of direct wages (Harrison and Reeve, 2002: 757). They differ from 'old' labour movements, in that they are not concerned with socioeconomic issues, but with 'post material' values related to lifestyle and 'identity politics' (G. Martin, 2015: 5). In the late 20th century, outside the traditional left/right political spectrum, new cleavages have emerged to address a wider range of social issues: '[a]nti-racists have pointed out that welfare services can be discriminatory and exclusive; disability campaigners have suggested that the needs of certain groups can be systematically ignored; and environmentalists have argued that existing service provision is predicated upon forms of economic development which cannot be sustained' (Alcock, 2012: 9). Communitarianism and third-way politics have heavily influenced conditional welfare reforms and the introduction of the private sector into public services. At the same time, these theoretical and political perspectives have led to the development of several urban regeneration initiatives in deprived areas and programmes aimed at tackling poverty. The initiatives build the conditions for autonomous development of the community and its citizens, emphasising the creation of opportunities for families and individuals to take part in collective activities and help them maintain relationships deemed essential for community well-being. Community action initiatives encourage and create conditions for social groups and associations to influence public decisions on the organisation of services, play an active role in the localisation of services and interventions and other aspects concerning their living conditions. The core belief of these initiatives is that a society exclusively based on market principles must be counter-balanced by the powers of a social state, a robust public sphere and a relationally sturdy civil society (Somers, 2008: 48).

Many years ago, the prominent sociologist Charles Wright Mills (1951) argued that 'there is no probability of the new middle class forming or inaugurating or leading any political movement'. The world has changed profoundly also in this aspect. Now, it is widely believed that the social basis of contemporary peace, environmentalist and feminist movements that are more inclined to be radically critical of the system are segments of the middle classes (Bagguley, 1995: 299; Giugni and Grasso, 2019).

Conclusion

This chapter has outlined major changes in the welfare attitudes of the middle class and the role played by self-interest, culture and values of ordinary people in making and implementing welfare programmes. The decades of welfare retrenchment after the economic crisis of the 1970s were crucial to a radical change of middle-class welfare attitudes. All European welfare states have been reconfigured towards progressive deregulation and privatisation of welfare policies, increasing state control over public welfare expenditure, and a stronger emphasis on the importance of individual choice and individual responsibilities. This trend towards individualised services responds to perceived competitive economic pressures (Farnsworth and Irving, 2015; Horsfall and Hudson, 2017) and to the needs and expectations of segments of the middle class who aspire to be creators of individual identity and authors of their lives. Beck and Beck-Gernsheim (2001: 23) highlighted that any attempt to create a new sense of social cohesion has to start from the recognition that individualism is written into Western culture and inevitably shapes public wishes and choices of policymakers.

As I have shown, the increasing level of conditionality placed on some groups deemed less deserving, the dualisation that affects the large majority of people and chauvinism, constitute key dimensions of the reforms planned by all European governments. The majority of social, economic and political actors think that being more selective, increasing the degree of conditionality and lowering the level of benefits for immigrants are priority measures. However, most European citizens defend a moderate position. Strict welfare chauvinism is clearly a minority position, and, on the contrary, the stance that newcomers should immediately be granted full access to benefits is endorsed by an equally small minority (European Social Survey, 2018). In all European countries, the need to distinguish between the deserving and undeserving poor emerges periodically, but from the 1980s onwards this distinction suggests strong pressures for a fundamental change of welfare and for rethinking several welfare priorities, programmes and areas of intervention.

In this chapter, I have argued that a large part of current welfare changes is increasing the hardship and instability experienced by the middle class and is not capable of managing more problematic low-income families. In many cases, highly individualised families do not have the relational resources to face economic deprivation and radical cultural changes. The impact on their living conditions is underestimated by policymakers and the majority of social and political actors.

These new politics of welfare affecting the middle class, mainly in terms of financial constraints and loss of social and economic security, contribute significantly to fuelling individual and collective radical activism and increasing instability in all European countries. In turn, many low-income families, minority ethnic groups and many more marginalised claimants are increasingly sanctioned or pushed out of welfare and the work system. Austerity and conditional welfare individualise the causes of unemployment and poverty and, rather than fostering the enhanced responsibilisation and self-reliance of claimants, risk promoting a further erosion of their security. Moreover, conditional welfare detaches from public welfare people who have more significant difficulties and persist in following reprehensible behaviours. Continuing from the age of dualisation, a 'third welfare system' ensured by charities is being strengthened, inhabited by social groups expelled from public welfare.

The welfare reforms promoted in all Western European countries are causing severe tension between globalisation winners and losers (Taylor-Gooby et al, 2017: 210). These reforms are intensifying the social division between more dynamic segments of the middle class (more educated and with higher socioeconomic status) and the lower middle class and low-income families. Wilensky noted that when the 'middle mass' looks up, it sees an overprivileged upper middle class and the rich who seem to evade taxes. When the 'middle mass' looks down, it sees the poor on benefits and immigrants whose moral lifestyle and ethnic–racial origin repel them, and whose children, they think, are at the root of crime and disorder (Wilensky, 2002: 394). From the middle of the 1970s onwards, Wilensky observed the increasing revolt of a segment of the middle mass against welfare. In recent years, a more extended individual and collective radical activism has emerged within a new middle mass, characterised by a confusing array of aspirations and resentments. The sense of indignation and anger emerging is increasingly difficult to govern without changing welfare institutions and strengthening their ability to reproduce and mobilise social resources.

5

A welfare for a highly individualised society

What does the middle class really need?

An active radical individualism of the middle class is emerging in a social context marked by differentiated relational and reflexivity resources and old and new risks. The weakness of rules and many integrative processes almost seem to detach the social relations of many groups from the world of institutions and create a multitude, a sort of middle mass, characterised by a not easily manageable individualism. Anger and resentment against the institutions and some target groups are forging the moral identities of this vast middle-class portion.

A large number of studies describe the link between radical activism of middle class and relative economic deprivation and cultural backlash. In the first chapter, I argued that all middle-class families can cope with income reductions and extensive cultural changes in broad terms. Deprivation and cultural changes create severe crises when other dynamics also play a critical role. The long-lasting transitions from first to second modernity is a context that creates other causal relations and strengthens the power causal relations of these dynamics. Specifically, with the erosion of the ordinary capacity of institutions and the fragmentation of the traditional and new social ties, many middle mass members cannot manage and address individually economic deprivations and the rapid changes in values.

To a different degree, in all Western European nations, the institutions seem incapable of inverting this seemingly irreversible trend and proposing collaborative identities, belonging and customs, making economic and political governance possible and fluid. The institutions are too often unable to address the major social challenges of individualised society.

The key issue is that societies cannot hope to govern anger and resentment against the institutions by creating new social divisions, increasing austerity in public spending and social control. This strategy works less and less with low-income households, and is not substantially applicable to the undisciplined activism of the middle classes. Too frequently it has counterintuitive effects and fuels radical right-wing or radical left-wing movements.

In Western Europe, the welfare state is focused on policies related to: work–family reconciliation; on containing the dramatic effects of relative economic deprivation; poverty and unemployment; the risks associated with an ageing population; and lack of self-sufficiency. The transformations that are taking place in family relations, anger and resentment against the institutions are deemed to be substantially restricted to some social groups and can be addressed by increasing control and surveillance and divisive and target systems of welfare.

In this chapter, I argue that it is possible to pursue a more inclusive, non-discriminatory and non-divisive social policy strategy overcoming some limitations of the prevailing frameworks in Europe. The starting point of this recalibration is the impact of the process of individualisation. This is to be understood as a structural dynamic of our societies that fragments social relations, but which can also be a challenge to renew individual and collective ties. As we have seen in Chapter 2, many authors argued that the process of individualisation can be understood as an ongoing social one, of 'disembedding', 'disenchantment', 'reintegration' and 'control'. The issue is that contemporary societies continuously promote new radical processes of 'disembedding' that span through all spheres of life, in informal relationships and economic and political institutions.

Welfare can promote 'embedding' processes and tackle the wholesale fragmentation of social relations by improving people's ability to work together for a common purpose and promoting extensive interventions in the quality of social life, strengthening civic values and trust in other people.

The current chapter highlights that it is necessary to carefully observe the complex nature of the transformations affecting the welfare–market–family relationships to improve welfare strategies appropriate for a competitive and globalised setting. Moreover, I outline some proposals for welfare reform, such as: a stronger public welfare, one which is grounded in the communicative sphere; activation programmes founded on a plurality of social resources; a relational state; and the need to support the new forms of social interaction that are emerging in all European countries.

Overcoming the divisive welfare state

The recalibrations of the programmes and instruments that were created in recent years (stricter and stronger politics of retrenchment, politics of austerity, new forms of dualisation, conditionality, progressive individualisation of the welfare services) do not seem able to cope with the changes in the living conditions of the majority of households. As we have seen in previous chapters, these changes worsen opportunities for the middle class to access both public and private welfare. Moreover, the emerging welfare system is not able to support a fully mobile individual that has internalised the market's needs and – regardless of social bonds – is willing to turn themselves into a flexible and mobile worker. It is not able to manage or include in shared strategies minority groups and 'undeserving' people.

Much research has documented the employment instability, economic deprivation and fragility of social networks and collective belonging of a large majority of people. The concerns of many middle-class households rise from the need to build one's future and the sensation of living in a condition of profound and growing uncertainty. For many social groups, the economic and care resources needed to face old and new risks have decreased significantly, and the existing welfare programmes appear less accessible and effective.

In many Western societies, a divided welfare state is consolidated. The three systems of welfare (social/public, fiscal and occupational) that Titmuss identified (1958), and the spheres of a mixed economy of welfare (public, private, voluntary and charitable sector, informal relations) are often not components of the same national welfare system: the interactions between them are becoming less and less significant. In many European countries, each of these spheres tends to constitute an autonomous and alternative system of welfare based on different logic and are aimed at addressing the needs of different groups: private welfare is the welfare of the established middle class; the public one is for the low middle and working class; and the charitable sector is there for the welfare of the more deprived groups.

In the UK, the government is seeking to change the direction of the welfare state from an engine of social cohesion to one of social division. The government adopts several tactics, including using social policy in a divisive way to advantage key groups of supporters and exclude and stigmatise non-supporters (Taylor-Gooby, 2016). The rise of insecure work, low-paid work and welfare reform (which has reduced social security entitlements and increased conditionality) are the key drivers of the rise of food charity in the UK (Lambie-Mumford, 2019). In Italy and Spain, many of the institutional and structural reforms undertaken by the welfare systems of Continental European countries were also adopted by the national welfare system: funded schemes for pensions, new forms of dualisation; the enhancement of the role of private actors in health care and welfare schemes on minimum income protection that reduce access to the benefits for immigrants and ethnic minorities. Many of these marginalised groups are 'expelled' from the welfare system benefits and turn to food charities.

In the Swedish welfare model, there are two very different systems: one, the public welfare state, is aimed at some social groups (the low middle and working class), while private welfare is aimed at other groups (the established middle class). There is often a gap between the two welfare states where many people tend to rely on charitable organisations (Lapidus, 2019).

In fact, what is emerging in all Western European countries is a welfare state where spending cuts in social expenditure have been accompanied by de-universalisation and extensive dualisation across many policy fields, an increase of state control over social care benefits and public health expenditure. Welfare is increasingly subordinated to the prevailing logics of economic development, and rather than counteract the effects of growing inequality, it is creating new social divides and new cleavages. Many kinds of divided welfare prevailing in Western Europe are part of an uncertain ongoing construction of new citizenship forms.

The changing relationship between public and private welfare provision provides for a limited area of intervention for public welfare and is aimed at a reduced number of beneficiaries. The impact on the middle class, mainly in terms of financial constraints, loss of economic security and economic opportunities and the risk of exposure to economic deprivation, is high and underestimated by policymakers and the majority of social and political actors. Palier (2012: 252) observes that in many countries such as Italy, Belgium, Germany and Austria, public pensions provided through social security will become so low that average-to-high earners will have to rely on occupational and private schemes to obtain a pension commensurate with their past earnings. This welfare system is closely linked to individualism's politics that combines a morality of individual responsibility with diminished support for collective provision; a divisive welfare state that enhances social division and undermines traditional class coalition that sustained welfare states (Taylor-Gooby, 2016).

Alcock calls for public welfare to meet our individual and social needs, and for state agencies to provide this because markets will not provide for all 'public goods'. The welfare state and the other spheres of life (third sector, market) are interdependent, not mutually exclusive. Private markets and voluntary action could never meet our needs for public goods without public investment and state action (Alcock, 2016: 11–12).

We need a welfare state that is able to create the economic and social conditions for supporting the autonomy of individuals. Individualised existences require a strong basic security net constructed by uniting different spheres such as institutional resources, informal care and social support relationships. Underpinned by core values such as respect, dignity and trust, it can strengthen civic values and rebalance the relationships between rights and obligations.

The social and cultural limits of the social investment approach

During the 1990s, new welfare strategies were introduced to face new social risks and ensure the welfare state's long-term sustainability. It was thought that the ageing demographics of Western Europe, changes in household structure, and negative effects of labour market dynamics were aspects of an irreversible transition to a post-industrial society, the impact of which could be mitigated by identifying new social policy solutions and renewed strategies able to reconcile social and economic goals.

The social investment approach has been the main attempt to reconceptualise the relationships between state, market and family; to reconcile economic growth with social inclusion, work with family life through investment in childcare and leave policies (Giddens, 1998; Bonoli and Natali, 2012; Morel et al, 2012). Overcoming the limits of the social protection approach that provides social insurance and social assistance for disadvantaged groups, the social investment is based on welfare as an investment in human and social capital. It aims to promote an active society capable of better addressing the new social risks and encouraging active participation in the mainstream of social and economic life (Esping-Andersen et al, 2002; Morel et al, 2012). The focus is to form high-quality human capital and public policies that prepare individuals, families and societies to adapt to transformations such as changing career patterns and working conditions or the development of new social risks (Morel et al, 2012: 354).

Social investment policies have assumed increasing prominence over the last three decades. Mahon (2013) argues that its initial formulations could be seen as an example of two different strategies: inclusive liberalism (gradual phaseout of benefits, the provision of wage subsidies, training and education) and intrusive liberalism that applies cuts in benefit rates, tightened eligibility requirements, short-term employability programmes and involves increased state surveillance over family survival strategies. Since then, however, this approach has begun to embrace important elements of a social-democratic strategy combining security for the workers and flexibility of the labour market, policies often termed 'flexicurity' (Mahon, 2013).

The experience of the four Scandinavian countries of Denmark, Norway, Sweden and Finland suggests that social investment policies can be a valuable way to reconcile protection and activation, and social and economic goals. These countries display high and broad-based education levels, which appear to translate into high levels of social capital and social cohesion, greater learning and innovation capacity at work, good economic growth including the creation of more and better jobs (Morel et al, 2013). In most European countries, social investment does not clearly propose a broader conception of social action and social inclusion different from neoliberal ideologies. In the UK, the strong emphasis on activation characterises the social investment perspective and justifies cutting back on benefits that previously allowed certain groups to remain outside the labour market (Morel et al, 2013). Though the social investment framework has gained particular prominence in the national political debate, most southern European countries have not applied this approach systematically and only in specific policy areas. In these countries, the social investment approach is unable to enhance a basic welfare security net to deal with the requirements of an individualised existence. In the last decade, in countries such as France, Belgium and the Netherlands, the pressures for retrenchment, dualisation in terms of access to services and spending cuts are stronger than the pressure for welfare state expansion on early childhood education and care and investment in human capital.

The relation between social investment-oriented policies and inequality variations has been the focus of a large part of the systematic and comparative empirical studies (Siza, 2019). Some research has claimed that there is no evidence that focusing on active social welfare and new social risks disturbs the egalitarian ambitions of the welfare state (Vaalavuo, 2013). In contrast, other authors note some evidence of a correlation between poverty and inequality variations and shifts in expenditure for social investment programmes (Cantillon 2011; Ghysels and Van Launcher, 2011; Van Vliet and Wang, 2015). In many cases, social investment programmes have created new forms of exclusion, new social divides and new stratifications rather than reduced inequality (Pintelon et al, 2013). While the impact of the transformation of the welfare state based on the social investment logic should not be underestimated, Van Kersbergen and Hemerijck (2012) argue that rising inequality has probably not been directly caused by this and that 'further empirical analysis is therefore needed' (p 489).

In the academic and public debate on social investment, other criticisms of this perspective are not adequately explored, although referring to central features and crucial dimensions of its conceptualisation. In particular, I am referring to work and family life reconciliation policies. Adopting a predominantly instrumental conception of individualisation and overcoming the traditional gender division of labour, the family is deemed a collection of individuals who have to compete in the labour market. Welfare is focused on family–market relationships and is mainly oriented to creating the conditions for helping employees to balance their work and family life. The attention paid to the quality of family ties and care relations in the private sphere declines. Most European governments now expect family policies to promote the participation of mothers in ever more flexible labour markets and facilitate the extension of the working life while attempting to remedy potential future labour and skill shortages (Daly, 2010). They adopt a conceptualisation of social citizenship that emphasises the validity of paid employment as central to its definition and as the primary obligation of citizenship, and undermines the value and legitimacy of informal care, the activities of parenting and other social obligations located in the private domestic as well as in the public sphere (Isin, 2008; Lister, 2011).

Although the social investment framework has produced positive changes in the welfare systems, this perspective tends to subordinate individual growth principles to the logic of the market and is exposed to frequent reductive implementations that unilaterally emphasise the economic dimensions of multidimensional concepts such as activation, defamilisation and active participation in social life. It no longer proposes a different human relations culture or a vision of future well-being in Western European societies; it does not speak to what we could become as individuals and communities. Social investment strategies emphasising the supply side (high-quality of human capital) need to be complemented by policies to promote good jobs for all. To be effective, social investment policies need to be accompanied by appropriate macroeconomic policies (Mahon, 2013).

Activation programmes founded on a plurality of social resources

Since the late 1980s, a spectre has been haunting Europe and beyond, the spectre of what may be called the 'active turn' to describe a direction of change that is nevertheless qualified in many ways (Hansen, 2019: 3–4). The 'active turn' has been applied to nearly all social policy from labour market policies to health, education, pensions, childcare and migration, always aiming to link social protection and labour-market participation (Barbier, 2005a).

All Western European countries have reoriented their welfare to promote social inclusion via employment, stressing relationships with the labour market and human capital investment, emphasising individual responsibility and behavioural changes in the most deprived social groups. Income protection measures are becoming less generous and increasingly dependent on obligatory activation programmes that, in many cases, substitute the income maintenance guarantees.

Many activation policies are associated with higher employment, but Active Labour Market Policies (ALMPs) via training are also linked to higher poverty (Taylor-Gooby et al, 2015: 100). The employment effects of activation policies on long-term unemployment depend on the institutional system of the labour market (Benda et al, 2020): they are much higher for those who receive unemployment benefits than those who receive social assistance (Larsen, 2005; J.P. Martin, 2015).

In recent years, the accelerating job polarisation between low-paying and high-paying occupations with the shrinking of middling occupations has profoundly changed the outcomes of the activation processes. Much research suggests that activation programmes are capable of supporting the active individual with high skills who can enter the job market quickly while experiencing increasing difficulties to improving the conditions of low-qualified workers with little or no work experience. Activation programmes meet similar difficulties in managing workers of middle-class segments with a low qualification level that have declining confidence in institutions, civic values and trust in other people.

Barbier (2005a) identified two distinct ideal types of activation. The 'liberal type' chiefly enhances the individuals' relationships to the labour market. ALMPs and social policies take on a limited role, restricted to inciting individuals to seek work, providing quick information and simple matching services, and investing in short-term vocational training. The second one is defined as 'universalistic' that caters to the provision of complex and extended services to all citizens but simultaneously guarantees relatively high living standards for the lower-paid sections of the labour force. Not systematically submitting citizens to work requirements, social policy retains its traditional contribution to well-being. Activation applies to all citizens in a relatively egalitarian manner, and the 'negotiating' between the individual's and society's demands appears much more balanced (p 115).

Adopting this perspective, we can take a further step towards activation programmes capable of recognising and mobilising the plurality of resources that the individual can dispose of in each sphere of life (informal relations, market, welfare). The desire to construct one's own life project should not be seen as an obstacle or constrained within standardised schemes but could be recognised instead as a real resource for an activation programme (Siza, 2019). This type of activation does not place into question the need to increase labour market participation but operates with the awareness that personal relationships, social networks and cultural capital are resources that can be decisive in social inclusion processes. If the real goal is the social integration of people, it is evident that the labour market cannot be the exclusive integrative resource.

A turn towards personalisation becomes crucial. Personalisation is defined as a mechanism that tailors services to the individual's specific circumstances, encompassing a wide diversity of initiatives (Needham, 2011: 43). A key element in this has been helping people to develop a network of support based on friendship and reciprocity, ascribing a strong role to families (Needham, 2011: 119). Growing social fragmentation could be dealt with through more personalised interventions, recognising care work in the family as equally important to paid work (Larsen, 2005). Equally, it could be contrasted by promoting activation programmes in which economic support is part of a broader aim to strengthen nets of social support and instil more confidence in institutions and a shared vision of the future. The aims of non-standardised activation measures could promote social inclusion, reinforce social ties and allow welfare beneficiaries to realise their projects, even if only partially. When possible, the measures targeted to an individual can be part of a collective project to regenerate a deprived area and to create the conditions for collaborative relationships and appropriate levels of communication between citizens and families.

A different relationship between state, market and informal sector

In Western Europe, since the 1980s, the support for a mixed economy of welfare has grown with the aim of integrating both the decrease of public resources along with the for-profit organisations and informal relation care resources. Evers defined the plural nature of the resources that contribute to welfare as 'the triangle of welfare' (1995). The role and the extent of these spheres of life have changed over time and from one context to another. Policies are shaped by the interaction among these spheres of life and the extension each represents in a specific context; they can make good or bad use of the resources each provides, recognise their presence, and enhance their autonomous capacity for initiative.

Many political and social actors consider these spheres of life as functional equivalents because they could be alternative ways to meet individual and collective needs. It is believed that welfare programmes sometimes can place greater emphasis on market resources, others on the voluntary organisations and community groups achieving seemingly similar outcomes. In fact, each mix we choose (more or less market, more or less informal relations) affects the direction of change, creates advantages or disadvantages for some social groups, and proposes different conceptualisations and operationalisations of individuals and collective well-being. Each sphere carries a conception of well-being and shapes the perceptions of actors. Their interactions limit the effects of unidirectional logic that distinguishes every single sphere (the market, the state, the third sector and the family).

For example, the risk for downward social mobility of an individual becomes very high when the crisis of the inclusive capacity of the work system is added to the low support and care capacity ensured by an unstable family and the frailty of friendship relations or by less protective welfare. Certain groups of people (low-income households, individuals with low levels of education, and people living in very disadvantaged communities) face a much higher risk when there are other disadvantages in their family and informal relations. Instead, in other social groups, one sphere of life compensates for the work system's weaknesses or pressure.

Welfare cannot simplify this setting: each sphere of life operates in any case, positively and negatively, influencing the dynamics of transformation even in situations in which the importance of the resources that it ensures are not recognised. A social action of one sphere inevitably falls in this interactive setting. Its probabilities of asserting its values and achieving its objectives depend on the kinds of interactions that emerge.

A mature welfare mix system recognises the plurality of resources and social autonomies that operate in well-being in the aforementioned three spheres of life. It can act as a process capable of valorising people's autonomous capacities and active participation. Through their involvement – their intentions, wishes and projects – it manages to change the functions and priorities of the public and private institutions.

In Western Europe, until the 1990s, the middle class built its integration on the solidity and stability of these three spheres of life (work, family, welfare).

Taken together, they ensured sufficient resources (fair paid work, welfare and stable family relations and predictable social support). For many years, the crisis of one sphere of life (growing labour market insecurity) was prevented thanks to the others (welfare and relative stable family relationships) avoiding deterioration of their living conditions.

In the last two decades, especially, the processes of individualisation have invaded all these spheres of life and the living conditions of the middle class without facing any cultural or social resistance. Individualisation has increased market dependency in all dimensions of life and has delivered the majority of people over to an external control and standardisation unknown in the enclaves of familial and feudal sub-cultures (Beck, 1992: 132). Individualised existence becomes dependent more and more on relations and conditions such as economic trends and the market dynamic far beyond individual control.

Several studies recognise the critical role that the market assumes in many societies. Somers (2008: 48) argues that the rise of market fundamentalism to the position of dominant ideational regime has created a radically unbalanced power dynamic between the market and state on the one side, and civil society on the other (Somers, 2008: 2). Democratic citizenship regimes require robust civil societies, which are deeply entangled with both the state and the market, while still doing the boundary work necessary to protect their own integrity. In civil society, social movements develop the capacities to pressure the state to build adequate social insurance programmes and non-contractual policies to protect against market-generated risks to health, retirement, education and social life (Somers, 2008: 48). The coordination of the market has the opposite consequence of disorganising the institutions of social integration (Browe, 2017: 95). Streeck (2016: 41) argues that social institutions are eroded by market forces and de-socialised capitalism hinges on the improvised performance of socially disorganised and politically disempowered individuals. Juul notes (2013: 138) that if instrumental rationality becomes totally dominant, nothing can prevent the mass production of inhumanity: modern culture contains a serious imbalance between norms concerning effectiveness and productivity on the one hand (for example, economic and administrative norms) and norms aimed at protecting the individual person on the other (that are ethical and legal norms. A relentless focus on material expansion is rendering non-market value such as care, human relations and community engagement as effectively 'value-less' (Bollier and Weston, 2013).

A crucial but unresolved question in the academic and political debate on family policies is which state or market relations can ensure individual independence from the family. Economic independence is often construed as commodification, that is, reliance on the market to provide an income as an alternative to depending on family members' economic support. In contrast, social independence is more often discussed as being achieved via state provision of services. The question of whether the state or the market are sources for independence from the family is not addressed explicitly in all concepts of defamilisation (Zagel and Lohmann, 2020: 136). Defamilisation is seen as a welfare policy that can lessen individual reliance on the family and aid the integration of women into the labour force (Esping-Andersen, 1999). Lister (1994) coined and defined this process as 'the degree to which individual adults can uphold a socially acceptable standard of living, independently of family relationships, either through paid work or through social security provisions' (1994: 173). The complementary concept of familisation refers to state support for care within the family and how the welfare state relies on the family as a welfare provider. It is losing relevance in the academic and political debate. In many cases, familisation is reductively described as the degree to which states increase social and economic dependencies between family members (Zagel and Lohmann, 2020).

Defamilisation is a complex process that values gender equality and labour participation. Still, it must be carefully defined to avoid sacrificing and not recognising the relevance of other values such as the expected reciprocity between members of the same family and care responsibilities.

We need a conceptualisation of state–market–family relationships that recognises that each sphere of life carries a different conception of care relations. In my perspective, family, state and market resources and action logics are not functional equivalents or functional alternatives, namely, equivalent ways to answer the same needs. Care and support relations ensured by a given sphere (for example, the family) can only be partially fulfilled by the other spheres (for example, the market). In terms of impacts on the quality of family relations, generous maternity and parental leave schemes are different from a system that ensures incentives to hire a care worker. Kinds of family support are different from those provided by residential care for the elderly and people with a disability, which completely lessen individual reliance on the family. Young children may not be largely defamilialised without depriving them of the possibility of developing meaningful and loving relationships (Saraceno and Keck, 2010: 691). There are key limitations with conceptualisations of defamilisation. We need to explore in much more detail how families practice reciprocity in, for example, forming intergenerational relationships of care among extended families, making intergenerational transfer of resources or goods (Papadopoulos and Roumpakis, 2019).

Policies are evaluated in terms of their impact on the conditions that favour or hinder participation in the labour market rather than in terms of their different impact on family relations, the family's ability to carry out all its functions, to create social capital, or to reduce its fragmentation and its instability.

New balances between individualised activism and collective bonds

Radical processes of individualisation are eroding the system and social integration of many European countries, and the capacity of collective institutions to manage and include active individuals that are disconnected from traditional forms of collective belonging. However, the process of individualisation includes both the removal from existing social forms and the 'reintegration dimension'.

Active welfare is dismantling traditional sectors and programmes but is not able to promote system and social reintegration for different groups and interests, nor is it able to promote shared norms and values and a social inclusion with equal rights for all social groups. What is evident is its incapacity to deal with the increasing instability of social relations and the apprehension that marks the lives of the majority of people.

Active social policy can contribute to rethinking the forms of sociality and the social ties that we can build in late modern life and support the new kinds of social support and new care relationships emerging in many spheres of life. In a highly individualised society, the task of an active welfare is to find a new balance, between individual actions and collective order, between risk and security, and to support new forms of social interaction and new ways of staying together.

As Beck and Beck–Gernsheim (2001) reminded us, it is possible to increase the degree of social integration in a highly individualised society if we can mobilise and motivate people to meet the challenges that lie at the centre of their lives. Where 'the social' is evaporating, society must be reinvented without suppressing the autonomy of individuals and by constructing conscious and more reflexive forms of 'detraditionalisation'.

Preview research highlights the emergence of new balances between individualised lives and collective bonds, which in some cases express an adaptation to a fluid society; in others, they interpret the widespread need of the majority of people for profound changes in the individualised and unstable social relationships. Human life is deemed liquid in many analyses, under constant change and transformation. Bauman (2003) believes that the individual is becoming an isolated monad in constant search of new models of sociability based on individualism, with weak and fragmented bonds, and notably with none of the fixed or durable bonds that would allow the effort of self-definition and self-assertion to come to a rest.

Spicker (2019) argues that in many cases, individualism and collectivism are two positions that could be held at the same time. People can have strong arguments for cooperation: people can agree to cooperate for mutual advantage, increase their capacity to share their risks, reduce their vulnerability; some things are only really possible if several people do them.

After all, individuals construct their sense of self and personal identity from their relationships with other people and their position in collective groups (pp 57–60). What kind of individualism and collectivism prevails in these cooperative actions, and which of them could be the basis for a new sociality and new welfare?

Empirical research has highlighted fluid forms of belonging and collective solidarity and the constant concern of many people to protect their individual independence. In a study situated in urban Stockholm, communal housing is framed as a case of 'individualised collectivism', a way of 'living alone together' which fosters moments of shared confidentiality and easily accessible sociability freed from suffocating dependencies. It is a flexible living that does not require an overabundance of emotional labour and lacks heavy dependency bonds (Törnqvist, 2019). In Israel, research has shown how members use the communal arena to express their individuality; they relate to the community as a site for the assertion of selfhood, though the self they celebrate is moulded by practices creating solidarity. The authors define the relation between individuality and solidarity as a 'collective of individuals' (Tavory and Goodman, 2009).

Communitarians and other movements outline a different balance between autonomy and collective belonging. In all communities, centrifugal forces seek to pull members out of their socially prescribed roles and duties towards their personal projects and centripetal forces that seek to absorb ever more psychic energy and resources into collective pursuits. Communities and individuals do best when these two forces are well in balance (Etzioni, 1995b: 19). A communitarian perspective recognises that the preservation of individual liberty depends on the active maintenance of the moral institutions of civil society (families, schools, communities of communities as voluntary associations). In these spheres, citizens learn respect for others and acquire a lively sense of their personal and civic responsibilities (Etzioni, 1995a). For regeneration of these institutions, conservatives seek to return to traditional life practices while the communitarians suggest new ones (Etzioni, 1996: 177).

In many parts of the world, forms of altruistic and cooperative ways of living have contributed to creating a new culture of human relations. There are a range of intractable social issues which are commanding an increasing share of national economies, many of which neither the market nor the existing model of public services has been able to solve. At the same time, there are an extraordinary number of new initiatives both from within the public sector and from households, cooperative society and voluntary organisations, which have created a great wave of alternative technologies and new forms of consumption and distribution (Murray, 2009). Key features of new approaches to care, education, welfare, food and energy are the intensive use of distributed systems; blurred boundaries between production and consumption; an emphasis on collaboration; and a strong role for personal values and missions (Cottam, 2011).

People express different forms of individualism, in many cases they are aware that there is an interaction between individual actions and structural pressures. Individual responsibility is inevitably shaped by constraints and objective conditions that can hinder or support a life project and that are not always modifiable through individual action (Archer, 2010).

However, although widespread, the new forms and resources of sociality among the people still do not seem capable of replacing strong traditional relationships of collaboration and belonging. Social policy can support the new kinds of social interaction and care relationships emerging in many spheres of life and contribute to rebuilding a sense of belonging and identity and harmonising autonomy and collective order. They can create the conditions for civil coexistence and provide vitality and sustenance to isolated individuals who lack trust in collective bonds.

Promoting an interplay between individual actions and institutions' activities

The twofold conception of society as both system integration and social integration could be the basis for a different welfare system able to promote a stronger institutional order and active communicative infrastructures (Lockwood, 1964; Habermas, 1984; 1987; Archer, 1996a; 1996b). In the last two decades, globalisation and radical processes of individualisation are eroding the system integration (at the level of macro-institutions), which arises from the interrelation of groups and collectivities and concerns the capacity of collective institutions to manage and include active individuals. There are growing institutional contradictions, problems of incompatibilities between differentiated sectors of welfare, economic, cultural and political systems, and the logic of the different institutionalised complexes of norms and roles.

More often, European societies present marked limitations regarding social integration, an integration based on intersubjective relations, interactions of familiarity and friendship. There are several critical issues in the social integration, conceived as a 'social space', the sphere of agency where different social activities are included in the system and exercise their actions mainly in face-to-face interaction between individuals or groups (Lockwood, 1964; Abbott et al, 2016). Social integration is judged by the extent to which social processes hold society together amicably or tend to divide groups and ultimately tear society apart (Abbott et al, 2016: 38). This distinction is an effective tool for a reconceptualisation of the relationships between state, market and family.

Although system and social integration are two distinct processes, they are necessary and inevitably connected to each other, albeit in permanent tension.

The main issue here is the need to adopt a welfare strategy capable of establishing an interplay between social integration and system integration. Such a strategy does not operate solely at the level of communicative relations and it is not a task that belongs only to the institutional sphere. Social integration and system integration do not merely coexist. Each system needs an external flow of arguments and ideas. Without consensus of the communicative sphere, no institutional system can adapt to their social environment; without the performance of the institutions, no communicative agreement can be stable. There is an interplay and an inclusive system integration does not ensure an inclusive social integration (Habermas, 1992; Brunkhorst, 2008).

Lockwood emphasised the distinction between social and system integration with the clear intent of increasing our ability to account for social change and to understand the causal power of the institution and communicative actions. Social antagonism of citizens is not a sufficient condition for changing a community when the system of institutions is well integrated free from tension or contradiction between its parts. Conversely, high contradictions and low integration between the institutions do not change a community or a society when no social agents are ready to exploit the system's integration. Stability and change rest upon the discrepancy between the properties of system integration and those of social integration (Lockwood, 1964; Archer, 1996b).

Historically, welfare programmes are founded on a combination of institutional and communicative resources, for example, in social care policies and the health sector where families' autonomous initiatives interact with the professional services. These processes can take place at the micro-level but include actions to coordinate or change the system of institutions. Integrating health and social care project built around frail older people's needs brings together institutions and structures, families and the voluntary sector. As Habermas (1984; 1987) pointed out, the market and the state are invading and undermining the integrative function of the realm of personal relationships. State and market deem to be stronger when they weaken and draw on the resources of the communicative infrastructure of the lifeworld, such as the family and informal social interactions. Communicative infrastructures were 'colonised' by the economy and the state, money and power (Habermas, 1987: 187). Colonisation forces adaptation of the lifeworld to system imperatives and imposes norms and values that are overwhelming the communicative resources of lifeworlds and the flow of communicative actions. The relevance of communicative actions in planning and delivering welfare resources is changing. Social integration is replaced by system integration: 'system mechanisms suppress forms of social integration even in those areas where a consensus-dependent coordination of action cannot be replaced, that is, where the symbolic reproduction of the lifeworld is at stake. In these areas, the mediatisation of the lifeworld assumes the form of a colonisation' (Habermas, 1987: 196). Social integration, rather than securing the socialisation of active individuals on the basis of communicative action, is becoming the principal victim of system imperatives. Habermas (1984; 1987) stresses the importance of the background of resources, relations, common beliefs, contexts and dimensions of social action in enabling institutions and individuals to integrate action. It is necessary and urgent to 'erect a democratic dam against the colonising encroachment of system imperatives on areas of the lifeworld' (Habermas, 1992: 444).

In recent decades, the 'colonisation' of the lifeworld has been increasingly undermining this sphere of life and creating imbalances and legitimation crises of the institutional order. This sphere is declining as a distinct realm; it no longer produces values and relations capable of influencing other spheres of life. What is affirmed is a sort of 'accumulation by dispossession' (Harvey, 2016): violent, predatory forms of accumulation such as consensus resources, wealth, social rights, and the commodification and privatisation of public goods, addressing individualisation processes towards competitive dimensions. As market conditions have prepared the ground for capitalism, a weakened family and social sphere is preparing the ground for a commercialised spirit of domestic life (Russel Hochschild, 2003: 13).

A welfare grounded on the realm of communicative actions

We need to counter these trends through a welfare system capable of strengthening the capacity of institutions both to reproduce and mobilise communicative resources. Bellah (1997: 388) claims that societies can never be based simply on a contract that maximises the opportunities of individuals. Individual opportunities are only possible in a modern society if they are balanced by community. Any group that seeks to maintain some continuity and coherence must also be a community, which means it must consider its institutional purposes and the values it gives meaning to.

Welfare institutions are often unable to reproduce and mobilise social resources, community relationships, and strengthen the family, friendships and the wider community to face the hardships and conflicts that develop within them. Moreover, they are unable to inspire community-based social change or promote local communities which are more sensitive to the common good.

The lifeworld remains as the only source of legitimation of public strategies (Habermas, 1987). In the last decade, welfare policies have become less and less anchored to communicative action. They are increasingly freed from contexts of the lifeworld and receive orientations, objectives and values from other spheres of life. The key values, principles and instruments of the active welfare state (human capital investment policies, equality of opportunity, and investment in childhood education activation policies) need to be rooted in the background of resources, relations, common beliefs, contexts and dimensions of social action that enable institutions and individuals to cooperate action (Habermas, 1984; 1987). In many welfare approaches, the structure of society is basically an interweaving of economics and politics with respect to which 'the rest', what lies outside the state–market pair, is not significant for the achievement of the common good, for citizenship, and for the workings of both market and state (Donati, 2021: 36).

However, these processes are not irreversible. It is necessary to discover the conditions that promote a civil coexistence that has at its base greater reciprocal trust, capable of giving vitality and sustenance to the institutions. The starting point is the assumption that collaborative relationships have not entirely vanished in the 'colonised lifeworld' and that they can be regenerated into the forms of communicative practices of self-determination (Habermas, 1996). As Habermas claimed, the main problem with society is maintaining and strengthening communicative action: the human species maintains itself through its members' socially coordinated activities, and this coordination is established through communication (1984: 397).

In all Western European countries, radical processes of individualisation have weakened the ties between individuals and their families and those with collective belonging. At the same time, these processes are often not creating shared forms of reintegration. Welfare programmes can have a crucial role in modifying the relationships between civil society and people who hold political, economic and social power positions. Welfare can effectively support people in taking collective actions to achieve the changes they desire and finding the resources they need to achieve their goals (Pitchford, 2008; Gilchrist, 2009). It can protect people against the growing risk of instability, promote well-being within the family, strengthen community relationships, and create neighbourhood communities more sensitive to the common good. Welfare can create the conditions for appropriate levels of communication between families, because an acceptable social life cannot be built in isolation.

We are all both receivers of care and givers of care. However, there are many situations where care is not seen as a public issue that calls for public policies. Social care is an area of policy that stands out as one where the roles and responsibilities of the different actors – state, market and citizens – are essentially interwoven with human relationships between families, friends and communities (Hill and Irving, 2020: 156).

We may assert that the welfare state, to be effective, will have to operate in the domains of system integration, especially within the context of robust market regulation (Diamond and Liddle, 2012: 289). At the same time, we need to overcome the exclusive market–state relation for promoting necessary changes in the realm of communicative actions. The welfare needs of the majority are changing, and the solutions proposed by social investment-oriented policies and other contemporary welfare systems appear less and less accessible and effective.

Bringing social back in the welfare state

In Western Europe, during the 1990s, new welfare systems were introduced to face new social risks and ensure the welfare state's long-term sustainability. In those years, the high fragmentation and instability of social relationships, the weakening of the ties between individuals and their families, were already evident. Many authors highlighted the growing fragmentation of social relations (Giddens, 1991; Beck, 1992; Etzioni, 1995). Other authors have outlined more radical transformation. Touraine deepens two main aspects of this issue: firstly, the decomposition of institutions and social actors who in the past were capable of transforming economic circumstances into social, collective events regulated by the state; secondly, the crisis of the social interpretation of historical facts and 'the death of the social' on the government strategies (Touraine, 1992). While a considerable amount of research has been published on the first topic, there is very little research on the second topic: the disappearance of the social from public strategies and the interpretation of their evolution.

Rose examined the latter topic in several influential books and articles. He argues that 'the social', as a plane of thought and action, has been central to political thought and political programmes since the mid-19th century (1999). Early modern societies became animated by a social way of thinking: 'the social' appeared as a 'distinctive idiom'. The nation must be governed in the interests of social protection, social justice, social rights and social solidarity (Rose, 1996: 329). Many reforms were promoted in the name of 'the social'. The target of these reforms was not simply to help the marginalised, but instead to strengthen the collective and to create better citizens, workers and parents (Rose, 1999). This particular enactment of 'the social' has dissolved during the last 20 years. 'Social' governmentality has come under attack from all sides of the political spectrum: it is no longer a key target of government strategies (Rose, 2008: 85; 1996: 327).

At the turn of the 19th and 20th centuries, 'the social' appeared as an antidote to individualisation and fragmentation (Rose, 1999), or as synonym of the collective. In his introduction to *Economy and Society* (1968), Weber distinguished between social and non-social action (p 26). What makes an individual's action social is that it is directed at someone or some other people. A social relationship is the behaviour of a plurality of actors for whom 'the action of each takes account of that of the others and is oriented in these terms' (quoted by Ahrne, 2021: 11).

'The social' in the sense in which it has been understood for about a century is nonetheless undergoing a mutation (Isin, 2008: 330). Isin (2008) noted that the social has dissolved into material logic and individualism; Dean (2020a) argues the culturally determined behaviours and socially constructed institutions that may humanise us can become dehumanising, eroding the relational needs for human contacts, interactions, belonging and love. Donati and Archer (2015; Donati, 2011) highlight a new macroscopic historical process of differentiation between 'the social' and 'the human': the detachment of 'the human' from 'the social' and an incursion of 'the inhuman' into its sphere. The 'social' becomes less and less 'human' because fundamental relations (such as of support, of care) are disappearing (Donati, 2011: 20–29).

Overall, all the authors discussed grasp the downgrading of 'the social' from public strategies, significant changes in collective values and people's willingness to relate. Atkinson et al (2017: 200) argue that what we call 'the social' has been hollowed out and downgraded in both policy and everyday life and excluded from the most important domains of our lives, public life and social institutions. Corbett and Walker emphasise the need to put 'the social' back into social policy (2017), promoting extensive interventions in the quality of social life, renewing the commitment to the community, collectively reconstructing conditions that promote an extended exploitation of its resources and its values, social bonds and memberships. The prioritisation of the economic understanding of human motivation and the downgrading of the social nature of human beings and their complex motivations are the key facets of neoliberal reductionism (Corbett and Walker, 2017), along with others, as well as their ability to deal with social risks.

Families and informal networks, collaborative and care relationships of households with formal services, networks of support, community organisations and social movements that represent the strength of 'the social universe' are fragmented and increasingly less relevant. This fragmentation favours the development of social policies in which market resources take on a prominent role. The twin logics of the market and the administrative political system organise welfare and social life according to their functioning and the imperatives of increasing their control power. Markets are shaping relationships more than welfare or the autonomous sociality of persons.

Moreover, the weakening of collaborative and care relationships produces increasingly uncertain outcomes of many welfare programmes, significantly reducing their efficacy. The initial design of many programmes and their recent recalibrations have underestimated the radical transformation of traditional social ties and seem neither able to cope with these radical transformations nor improve people's ability to work together for a common purpose. In family relations and in communities, several critical issues are emerging and tend to be more significant: the weakening of the availability of social resources, collective subjects, and care and collaborative relations needed to plan and implement welfare programmes.

The compatibility of current working conditions with family life is diminishing. The quality and intensity of informal care find itself in constant competition with the need to participate in the labour market (Brimblecombe et al, 2017; European Commission, 2018a). This, in turn, requires processes of defamilisation even in the absence of appropriate supportive care policies and work–life balance policies. During the last decade, it has become less likely that social policies to lessen individual reliance on the family are able to produce the expected outcome in terms of family well-being, individual social independence and proper early childhood education. Measures to enable women (and men) to perform the role of a family carer and maintain a reasonable standard of living (such as care-related leave, policies to increase the quality or availability of flexible and alternative work arrangements) increasingly do not cope with a risk produced by non-standard forms of work and changing demands for skills in the workplace (Saxonberg, 2013; Chau et al, 2016; European Commission, 2018b; 2018c).

Addressing resentment against institutions

Welfare can play an essential role in our societies when it aims to create opportunities for families and individuals to take part in collective activities and help them build and maintain relationships deemed crucial for the community's well-being. It can support people to take collective actions to achieve the changes they desire and find the resources to achieve their goals (Pitchford, 2008; Gilchrist, 2009). Additionally, welfare can encourage and create conditions for social groups and associations to influence public decisions on the organisation of services and participate in co-creative processes strengthening the social cohesion of the individualised society.

A considerable amount of literature has grown up around a system of welfare promoting a social safety net and quality health and education institutions; it is a welfare that promotes relational outcomes beyond conditional welfare or systems that neglect the importance of human relationships. Key drivers of this welfare are participation, equal access to services and inclusive citizenship. It is founded on a collaborative approach, collective relationships and supports citizens' resources and capabilities.

For many authors, the Nordic welfare state is a relational system that adopts a collaborative approach premised on human rights, social justice and sustainable societal development (Ness and Heimburg, 2021: 36). Nordic welfare as a whole is understood as a complex web of relations bound together by trust practices (Hänninen et al, 2019: 2). More radically, there are many local experiences where, in a relational process, the involvement of individuals co-creates the priorities, the direction and the functions of public and private institutions. Community development (Henderson and Thomas, 2013), community practice (Butcher, 2007), relational welfare (Cottam, 2011) and participatory social policy (Beresford, 2016) can be relevant approaches for engaging and achieving collaborative and responsible communities (Banks, 2007: 78) avoiding low-income households from being held back from participating fully. Hillary Cottam (2011: 134) argued that the current parameters of the debate around welfare reform are inadequate:

> A relentless focus on finance and costs has obscured the systemic challenges facing our post-war welfare institutions. Although exacerbated by the current financial crisis, these challenges have deeper roots, and are as much about culture, systems and relationships as they are about money. When we look through the eyes of those families most reliant on the welfare state we can better understand the nature of problem. (Cottam, 2011: 134)

It is also necessary to discover what gives vitality and sustenance to the different parts of the state, the conditions that promote civil coexistence with greater reciprocal trust at its base. To counter the rise of resentment against the institutions among the middle and the working class, many authors highlight the need for a state in which citizens have a voice in policymaking. A relational state that supports active welfare and ensures collaboration in the implementation of inter-sectoral welfare programmes and synergy between social, economic and cultural resources.

The relational state seeks to enable citizens to solve their own problems through association with others and encourage them to collaborate with all institutions (Cooke and Muir, 2012). The procedural fairness of institutions influences citizens' institutional trust and, more specifically, how citizens experience feelings of safety and protection (Rothstein and Stolle, 2008: 456). The relationships between the government and the governed are circular or recursive.

In addition to seeking higher standards in education and in health services or lower crime rates, governments should aim to improve both the quality of their relationship with citizens and the relationships between citizens. Broadening and deepening relationships should be seen as an outcome to which the state should aspire (Mulgan, 2012).

> If the delivery state assumed largely atomised and passive citizens, often described as consumers, the relational state concerns itself with encouraging, supporting and rewarding citizens coming together to get things done. Instead of a linear delivery model, the government moves to a more two-way relationship with citizens and encourages citizens to collaborate. (Mulgan, 2012: 25)

For these authors, the relational state is characterised by its ability to articulate social interrelationships by producing and spreading information, raising society's awareness of its responsibility, promoting social self-regulation, and acting as an intermediary between different social actors. Other authors highlight that the legitimacy of the relational state stems from its capacity for dialogue and openness towards different social actors and its ability to foster social inclusion (Mendoza and Vernis, 2008: 393). The relational state seeks to achieve the greatest possible synergy between the resources, the system and social integration; it locates the relations between the state, the market and civil society in the field of co-responsibility, which is a crucial but missing feature in the neoliberal state and the welfare state models (Mendoza and Vernis, 2008: 390).

Welfare that is active, participatory, relational and able to reproduce and mobilise social resources can be focused on new challenges that are transforming contemporary societies. These challenges are especially noticeable in the middle of social stratification where a sort of multitude is emerging which has a scarcely defined social identity and weak social bonds, which shares conditions of economic difficulty, and feels unable to deal with the new risks of a globalised society. This welfare can effectively contribute to the construction of better relationships and a better society. Abbott et al (2016) identify four social processes necessary to create a society able to offer a decent life to its members and ensure that all of its people can exercise their human rights: economic security; social cohesion; social inclusion; and empowerment. All four processes call for a decisive contribution from welfare. The central focus of economic security is managing risk and creating life chances: if economic survival is precarious, strategies have to be in place to deal with sudden shortfalls, and resources have to be supplied reliably. Social cohesion is the glue holding societies together: solidarity and shared norms and values, the extent to which individuals and groups of people share social relations and groups with different interests tolerate each other. Social inclusion is the basis for participating in the social, economic, political and cultural institutions of a society. Empowerment is providing what is necessary for people to exercise agency and act autonomously (Abbott et al, 2016: 16–18). A 'decent society' where everyone has enough to eat, where there are sufficient resources to cushion people against sudden emergencies, where people are able to trust each other and institutions, where all residents are treated more or less as citizens and there is no second-class groups of slaves, serfs or mere workers, where people can acquire and use capabilities freely provided their doing so does not constrain the freedom of others (Abbott et al, 2016: 146).

The welfare that aims to respond to these needs radically differs from the divisive forms adopted by all European governments. It is welfare capable of mobilising the resources of all spheres of life – informal relations, public and private systems, and the third sector – and combining them not in a divided welfare system but in a strategy able to protect the established middle class and minority ethnic groups and promote opportunities to make better lives for them.

Conclusion

In this chapter, I argued that in all European countries, to different degrees, welfare institutions cannot manage the radical transformation of traditional and new social ties and the loss of economic security of the majority of people. Welfare institutions with increasing difficulty support the middle class's capacity to fit into an active and dynamic economic process through their own personal commitment.

In the chapter, I argue that it is possible to pursue a more inclusive social policy strategy. It may be a welfare configuration capable of protecting people against the growing risk of instability and to contribute to the rebuilding of a sense of belonging and identity. Welfare can act as a process capable of recognising the activism and autonomous capacities of people, and can contribute towards supporting the new kinds of social interaction and new care relationships that are emerging in many spheres of life.

A reconceptualisation of the relationships between state, market and the informal sector can help us recognise the plurality of resources that the individual can dispose of in each sphere of life (informal relations, market, welfare) and promote new welfare strategies. Different individuals and social groups draw on different levels and combinations of the resources provided by these spheres to manage their lives. Adopting this approach, I have outlined some proposals to change key welfare programmes and to create more collaborative relations of welfare institutions both with the majority of people and with minority groups.

I have further taken into account the twofold conception of society as both system integration and social integration to promote institutional programmes more grounded in the communicative sphere, a relational state, as well as activation programmes founded on a plurality of social resources. Middle-class disenchantment and its profound distrust of major social and political institutions could be dealt with through more personalised activation programmes. The aim is to support new forms of altruistic and cooperative processes of individualisation that can create a new culture of human relations.

Conclusion: The 'worlds' of welfare and the divided middle class

The key points in my analysis

In the last two decades, in all Western European countries, active welfare reforms and 'hidden politics' (budget cuts, nondecisions, partial implementation of public programmes) have promoted de-universalisation and extensive dualisation across many policy fields and a stable rebalancing of the institutional relationships between public and private welfare. The previous chapters highlight that reforms and recalibrations are underpinned by a partial understanding of the living conditions of a large part of the middle class and low-income households. The widespread belief among political and social actors is that a considerable part of the middle class can invest a portion of its income to access effective and high-quality private health services or private pension schemes. Welfare is tailored to an active and individualised family that can turn to private systems to meet its main healthcare, education and long-term care requirements. For low-income households, it is assumed that many of them do not deserve the benefits they receive and do not do everything they can to find work. The priority of many European governments is to discipline the behaviour of welfare claimants and to increase control and surveillance in the neighbourhoods where they live.

The attitudes and living conditions both for low-income households and middle classes are very different from how they are recognised and discussed in public debate. The growth of informal work and low-paid jobs is devasting for people living on low incomes. Cuts in public expenditure and the punitive welfare turn promote a further erosion of their stability. Rather than enhancing the responsibility and self-reliance of the welfare claimants, these welfare recalibrations increase their resentment against institutions.

For the middle class the vast majority of all upward mobility opportunities have decreased in almost all European countries. The middle class has lost job security and income has slowly decreased: social mobility is often not the reward for hard work. In all European countries, only some middle-class segments have registered an improvement in their condition in the last two decades and occupy social positions that provide them with material and cultural advantages. Intergenerational mobility is low and for lower-income households becoming middle class is increasingly difficult. In Denmark, for a person to rise from lower to middle income takes on average about two generations; in the UK and the US it takes five; in Spain four and in countries such as France and Germany, it takes more than six generations (Shafik, 2021: 8–9).

The limitations of the employment structure are often hidden. Great upward mobility requires more destinations that can receive the upwardly mobile (Lawler and Payne, 2018: 21). The polarisation of the labour market between the increase of low-paying and slight increase of high-paying occupations and the shrinking of middle-paying occupations do not allow more mobility in the UK and all Western Europe countries.

A considerable amount of research highlights the 'middle-class squeeze' (Kus, 2013). The economic insecurity of the middle class and its heightened sense of precarity have widespread consequences not only for the quality of jobs, but also on many other outcomes of personal well-being, family and community life, voters' behaviour, support for universal benefits in welfare, and trust in institutions (Kallenberg, 2018). The middle class feels that the current socioeconomic system is unfair, its lifestyle is increasingly expensive, and income prospects are increasingly uncertain and more susceptible to suffering from increasingly unstable conditions (Eurofound, 2015; OECD, 2019: 28–29; European Commission, 2020).

However, in many chapters, I argued that the middle-class decline and its radicalisation cannot be conceptualised only in terms of economic inequality or cultural changes. Relative economic deprivation certainly plays a critical role in the radicalisation of middle-class activism and much research highlighted empirical regularities between these dynamics. However, as Bhaskar (2008) reminded us, only one of the several mechanisms affecting this outcome is being researched. Instead, there is a 'multiple determination' of a single event and the context can hinder or increase the generative capacity of a single causal relationship. The reality is constituted not only by experiences and the course of these actual events, but also by powers, mechanisms and tendencies that underpin, generate or facilitate the phenomena that we may (or may not) experience (Bhaskar and Lawson, 1998: 5).

In this perspective, I try to understand the complex nature of the changes affecting the middle class and its radical activism, focusing on interactions between the economic and cultural 'change mechanisms' highlighted by the well-established research and the set of causal power relations existing in the context that are inevitably involved in co-determining the outcome. In every context, constraints and objective conditions hinder or support individual actions and shape individual responsibility.

Referring to these interactions provides a more comprehensive understanding of the middle-class welfare needs and contributes to identifying the integrative resources that we can mobilise to counter or mitigate the negative impacts of economic deprivation and radical cultural changes.

No one is ever safe alone

The book aims to contribute to ongoing public and academic debates about social and political instability and the unpredictability of the majority of attitudes and behaviours in both the public and private spheres of life. In Chapter 2, I argued that we can capture the real impact of the changes on social life within a contextual setting firmly shaped by radical processes of individualisation. These processes, intensified by globalisation and technological changes, have radically transformed the foundations of everyday life.

In the current highly individualised setting, economic deprivation and cultural changes are perceived and dealt with by individuals with weaker social networks and collective belonging. Their relative deprivation is mostly experienced individually by seeking biographical solutions to systemic contradictions. A large part of the middle class is more concerned about the future and current institutions that struggle to manage old and new risks. Unlike the traditional middle class, many segments of this class do not share a collective project of upward mobility but individual projects and individual responsibility to improve their living conditions. An increasing social differentiation in ordinary life, personal resources and relationships is accompanied by a standardisation of social expectations, cultural references and life projects.

Individuals can independently manage their own personal growth, obtaining advantages and higher degrees of freedom than those obtainable in past static societies.

Over the last ten years, the situation has changed dramatically: a radical imbalance is emerging between the growing individual risks (unemployment, precarity, instability and loosening of informal ties) on the one side, and decreasing opportunities on the other. The newly acquired universes of values are no longer compatible with the instability of the employment sector, economic difficulties and the fragility of social networks. The atomisation and isolation of individuals become more frequent than the open and dynamic kinds of sociality that the second modernity promised.

Processes of individualisation cross every social context and interact with existing market subjects, the state, informal resources and with the social action of reflexive individuals. These processes freed a very large mass of individuals from old and new ties, collective belonging, stable values and promoted, at the same time, new social aggregations and associative forms much less stable, fragile, transient and under constant transformation. What is emerging is a multitude of people without stable belonging and life projects that can steer the new forms of sociality towards a credible social position. It is a 'new middle mass' because it mainly includes the middle and working classes, in other words, the majority of people rather than minority groups and the most deprived households.

This new stratum looms over political and social debate. This stratum is characterised by a confusing array of aspirations, contradictory values and intolerance towards rules and belonging. Resentment against the institutions and some target groups (ethnic minorities and traditionally undeserving groups) are forging its moral identity. It ensures collective support for configurations of divisive welfare (welfare chauvinism and welfare conditionality) and has conflictual relations with welfare institutions. The increasing level of conflict manifested in care relationships (that is, in doctor–patient relationships and the emergence of 'defensive medicine') highlights how several critical changes that have taken place in the social fabric are invading and undermining the institutions. The same is true for the difficulties experienced in identifying shared innovative solutions to create opportunities for families and individuals to participate in collective activities and play an active role in many aspects of their living conditions. All different 'worlds' of welfare states seem progressively less capable of addressing the new needs and preferences of a large portion of the middle class, especially the lower segment, and managing attitudes of resentment and radical forms of individualism.

However, individualisation means, first, the disembedding of industrial society ways of life and, second, the re-embedding of new ones in which the individuals must produce, stage and cobble together their biographies and find and invent new certainties (Beck, 1997: 95). In the last two decades, institutions, intermediate organisations and communities face increasing difficulty in identifying forms of social integration and actions and resources for supporting the new emerging forms of sociality and care relationships. Each new cleavage and social division tries to impose a social identity, rules and models of life they share; at the individual level, everyone has difficulties accepting different styles of life and even the smallest inequality.

A transition towards an inclusive welfare?

We are experiencing a long-lasting transition from a simple modern society to a complex modern society that simultaneously and radically fragments the social fabric and destabilises all certainties. In turn, the uncertain and contradictory responses of institutions and most social and economic subjects make this transition particularly complex. It is difficult to govern the anger and resentment against institutions felt by the majority by increasing social control, austerity, welfare fragmentation and social divisions. In all European countries, by neglecting the distributional effects of benefits and services, the welfare state is generating the phenomenon that Merton (1968) called 'the Matthew effect': the initial advantage tends to beget further advantage, and the initial disadvantages beget further disadvantages (Rigney, 2010: 1), widening the social divisions between established middle class, the middle and working classes and low-income households. The recalibrations of welfare programmes created in recent years do not seem to cope with the extended changes we are living.

In recent years, the welfare that the middle class can access is no longer the same as the system during the era of major welfare expansion (1960–1975), that tended to ensure generous benefits (higher quality of services in areas such as health, pensions, childcare and education) for the middle classes. The current welfare is strongly weakened by stricter politics of retrenchment, politics of austerity and new forms of dualisation, leading to the fact that the vast majority of the middle class has insufficient protection through public services and limited access to private insurance. The welfare of the vast majority of the middle class is different to the welfare of the middle-class segment with a higher socioeconomic status who primarily benefit from adequate public and private protection (such as private health insurance, a private education system, private old-age pensions) and occupational schemes, being able to face old and new social risks.

The current welfare of the middle class is also not the welfare of the long-term unemployed, minority ethnic groups, low-income families with children, social tenants and the homeless. It is not a conditional welfare that combines sanctions, financial penalties and support to change the behaviour of welfare recipients or a 'welfare chauvinism' that restricts access to benefits or lowers the level of benefits for immigrants and ethnic minorities.

Welfare system preference is becoming part of middle-class distinction strategy and one dimension of Bourdieu's concept (1987) of social and cultural capital. Welfare preference is the product of education, anchored in the systems of perception and action that distinguish a class or a cleavage and contribute to creating a sense of collective identity and defending a relatively privileged social position. However, the middle class is increasingly fragmented: a large part supports the divisive welfare systems, another part supports an inclusive welfare and is against social divisions, inequality and all class distinction strategies. The former strongly supports every retrenchment strategy that restricts social benefits to members of the native group and cuts benefits for undeserving claimants and immigrant populations. The latter constitutes the main social basis of many contemporary movements fighting for social justice for refugees and migrant workers with the aim to strengthen civic values and trust in other people. Their activism around disability, sexual citizenship, rights for carers and children influenced pressure-group activity and was reflected in social policy practices (Williams, 2021). New collaborative relationships, new opportunities for social dialogue and alternative ways of looking at the world are emerging within these middle-class segments.

Welfare can act as a process capable of recognising this activism and autonomous capacities of people and can contribute to supporting the inclusive kinds of social interaction emerging in many spheres of life. A civil coexistence that has greater reciprocal trust as its base could give vitality and sustenance to individuals who are isolated and lacking trust in collective bonds.

The long-lasting transition that we are experiencing could likely have very different outcomes; in the short term, creating profound disorientation and a very extensive social crisis, but in the long run potentially allowing the development of new collaborative relationships, and providing different ways of imagining social integration.

I strongly believe that pursuing a more inclusive, non-discriminatory and non-divisive social policy strategy is possible. In other words, it may be a welfare configuration capable of protecting people against the growing risk of instability. Individualised existences require a stronger basic security net designed to meet basic needs, an increased access to education and quality health institutions, and fair pension schemes. Moreover, we need these stronger public provisions and services to become more responsive, open and accountable to the citizenry (Banks et al, 2003). This welfare system needs to give communities and service users a greater say in the design and delivery of public services (Gilchrist and Taylor, 2022); it needs to reproduce and mobilise social resources and community relationships as well as committing to supporting individuals' autonomy and steering individual life projects towards cooperative and altruistic ends.

References

Abbott, P., Wallace, C. and Sapsford, R. (2016) *The Decent Society: Planning for Social Quality*, London: Routledge.

Abel-Smith, B. (1958) 'Whose welfare state?' in N. Mackenzie (ed) *Conviction*, London: MacGibbon and Kee, pp 55–73.

Ahrne, G. (2021) *The Construction of Social Bonds*, Cheltenham: Edward Elgar.

Alcock, P. (2012) 'The subject of social policy' in P. Alcock, M. May and S. Wright (eds) *The Student's Companion to Social Policy*, Oxford: Blackwell, pp 5–11.

Alcock, P. (2016) *Why We Need Welfare*, Bristol: Policy Press.

Alexander, J.C. (1983) *The Modern Reconstruction of Classical Thought: Talcott Parsons*, Berkeley: University of California Press.

Algan, Y., Guriev, S., Papaioannou, E. and Passari, E. (2017) 'The European trust crisis and the rise of populism', *Brookings Papers on Economic Activity*, 48(2), pp 309–400.

Andersen, J.G. and Bjørklund T. (1990) 'Structural changes and new cleavages: The progress parties in Denmark and Norway', *Acta Sociologica*, 33(3), pp 195–217.

Annetts, J., Law, A., McNeish, W. and Mooney, G. (2009) *Understanding Social Welfare Movements*, Bristol: Policy Press.

Antonucci, L., Horvath, L., Kutiyski, Y. and Krouwel, A. (2017) 'The malaise of the squeezed middle: Challenging the narrative of the "left behind" Brexiter', *Competition and Change*, 21(3), pp 211–229.

Archer, M. (1996a) *Culture and Agency*, Cambridge: Cambridge University Press.

Archer, M. (1996b) 'Social integration and system integration: Developing the distinction', *Sociology*, 30(4), pp 679–699.

Archer, M. (2003) *Structure, Agency and the Internal Conversation*, Cambridge: Cambridge University Press.

Archer, M. (2007) *Making Our Way Through the World: Human Reflexivity and Social Mobility*, New York: Cambridge University Press.

Archer, M. (2010) *Conversations About Reflexivity*, New York: Routledge.

Arendt, H. (1951) *The Origins of Totalitarianism*, New York: Harcourt Brace.

Armingeon, K. and Ceka, B. (2013) 'The loss of trust in the European Union during the great recession since 2007: The role of heuristics from the national political system', *European Union Politics*, 15(1), pp 82–107.

Arndt, C. (2019) 'The middle class in Germany' in A. Siegmann (ed) *The Middle: The Middle Class as the Moral Core of Society*, Brussels: Wilfried Martens Centre for European Studies, pp 35–52.

Atkinson, A.B. (2015) *Inequality: What Can Be Done?*, Cambridge, MA: Harvard University Press.

Atkinson, R., Mckenzie, L. and Winlow, S. (eds) (2017) *Building a Better Society*, Bristol: Policy Press.

Badie, B., Berg-Schlosser, D. and Morlino, L. (eds) (2011) *International Encyclopaedia of Political Science*, Thousand Oaks: SAGE.

Bagguley, P. (1995) 'Middle-class radicalism revisited' in T. Butler and M. Savage (eds) *Social Change and the Middle Class*, London: Routledge, pp 293–309.

Baldwin, P. (1990) *The Politics of Social Solidarity: Class Bases of the European Welfare State, 1875–1975*, Cambridge: Cambridge University Press.

Banks, S. (2007) 'Working in and with community groups and organisations: Processes and practice' in H. Butcher, S. Banks and P. Henderson (eds) *Critical Community Practice*, Bristol: Policy Press, pp 77–96.

Banks, S., Butcher, H., Henderson, P. and Robertson, J. (2003) *Managing Community Practice*, Bristol: Policy Press.

Barbehön, M. and Haus, M. (2015) 'Middle class and welfare state discursive relations', *Critical Policy Studies*, 9(4), pp 473–484.

Barbehön, M., Geugjes, M. and Haus, M. (2020) *Middle Class and Welfare State: Making Sense of an Ambivalent Relationship*, London: Routledge.

Barbier, J.C. (2005a) 'Citizenship and the activation of social protection: A comparative approach' in J.G. Andersen, A.M. Guillemard, P.H. Jensen and B. Pfau-Effinger (eds) *The Changing Face of Welfare: Consequences and Outcomes from a Citizenship Perspective*, Bristol: Policy Press, pp 113–134.

Barbier, J.C. (2005b) 'The European employment strategy: A channel for activating social protection?' in J. Zeitlin and P. Pochet (eds) *The Open Method of Coordination in Action: The European Employment and Social Inclusion Strategies*, Brussels: PIE-Peter Lang, pp 417–466.

Bartolini, S. (2011) 'Cleavages, social and political' in B. Badie, D. Berg-Schlosser and L. Morlino (eds) *International Encyclopaedia of Political Science*, Thousand Oaks: SAGE, pp 276–282.

Bartolini, S. and Mair, P. (1990) *Identity, Competition, and Electoral Availability: The Stabilisation of European Electorates, 1885–1985*, New York: Cambridge University Press.

Bauman, Z. (1998) *Work, Consumerism and the New Poor*, Buckingham: Open University Press.

Bauman, Z. (2000) *Liquid Modernity*, Cambridge: Polity Press.

Bauman, Z. (2001) *The Individualised Society*, Cambridge: Polity Press.

Bauman, Z. (2003) *Liquid Love: On the Frailty of Human Bond*, Cambridge: Polity Press.

Beck, U. (1992) *Risk Society: Towards a New Modernity*, London: Sage.

Beck, U. (1997) *The Reinvention of Politics*, Cambridge: Polity Press.

Beck, U. (2000) *The Brave New World of Work*, Cambridge: Polity Press.

Beck, U. (2016) *The Metamorphosis of the World*, Cambridge: Polity Press.

Beck, U. and Beck-Gernsheim, E. (1995) *The Normal Chaos of Love*, Cambridge: Polity Press.

Beck, U. and Beck-Gernsheim, E. (2001) *Individualisation*, London: Sage.

Beck, U. and Grande, E. (2010) 'Varieties of second modernity: The cosmopolitan turn in social and political theory and research', *The British Journal of Sociology*, 61(3), pp 409–442.

Beck, U. and Lau, C. (2005) 'Second modernity as a research agenda: Theoretical and empirical explorations in the "meta-change" of modern society', *The British Journal of Sociology*, 56(4), pp 525–557.

Beck, U. and Willms, J. (2004) *Conversation with Ulrich Beck*, Cambridge: Polity Press.

Beck, U., Bonss, W. and Lau, C. (2003) 'The theory of reflexive modernisation: Problematic, hypotheses and research programme', *Theory, Culture and Society*, 20(2), pp 1–33.

Becker, S.O., Fetzer, T. and Novy, D. (2017) 'Who voted for Brexit? A comprehensive district-level analysis', *Economic Policy*, 32(92), pp 601–651.

Beider, H. (2015) *White Working-class Voices*, Bristol: Policy Press.

Beider, H. and Chatal, K. (2020) *The Other America: White Working Class Perspectives on Race, Identity, and Change*, Bristol: Policy Press.

Bellah, R.N. (1997) 'The necessity of opportunity and community in a good society', *International Sociology*, 12(4), pp 387–393.

Bellah, R.N., Madsen, R., Sullivan, W.M., Swidler, A. and Tipton, S.M. (1996) *Habits of the Heart: Individualism and Commitment in American Life*, Berkeley: University of California Press.

Benda, L., Koster, F. and Van Der Veen, R. (2020) 'Activation is not a panacea: Active labour market policy, long-term unemployment and institutional complementarity', *Journal of Social Policy*, 49(3), pp 483–506.

Bennett, T., Savage, M., Silva, E. Warde, A., Gayo-Cal, M. and Wright, D. (2009) 'Culture, class, distinction', *The British Journal of Sociology*, 60(4), pp 835–836.

Beresford, P. (2016) *All Our Welfare: Towards Participatory Social Policy*, Bristol: Policy Press.

Berger, S. (2017) 'Populism and the failures of representation', *French Politics, Culture & Society*, 35(2), pp 21–23.

Bermeo, N. and Bartels, L.M. (eds) (2014) *Mass Politics in Tough Times: Opinions, Votes, and Protest in the Great Recession*, New York: Oxford University Press.

Betz, H.G. (1993) 'The new politics of resentment: Radical right-wing populist parties in western Europe', *Comparative Politics*, 25(4), pp 413–427.

Betz, H.G. (1994) *Radical Right-wing Populism in Western Europe*, New York: St Martin's Press.

Betz, H.G (2004) *Exclusionary Populism in Western Europe in the 1990s and Beyond: A Threat to Democracy and Civil Rights? Identities, Conflict and Cohesion*, Programme Paper No. 9, United Nations Research Institute for Social Development.

Bhaskar, R. (1979) *The Possibility of Naturalism: A Philosophical Critique of Contemporary Human Sciences*, Brighton: The Harvester Press.

Bhaskar, R. (2008) *A Realist Theory of Science*, 3rd edition, Abingdon: Routledge.

Bhaskar, R. and Lawson, T. (1998) 'Introduction: Basic texts and developments' in M.S. Archer, R. Bhaskar, A. Collier, T. Lawson and A. Norrie (eds) *Critical Realism: Essential Readings*, London: Routledge, pp 3–15.

Bigot, R., Croutte, P., Muller, J. and Osier, G. (2012) *The Middle Classes in Europe, Evidence from the LIS Data*, working paper series, nr. 580, Luxembourg: Luxembourg Income Study (LIS).

Blyth, M. (2015) *Austerity: The History of a Dangerous Idea*, Oxford: Oxford University Press.

Bollier, D. and Weston, B. (2013) *Green Governance: Ecological Survival, Human Rights and the Law of the Commons*, New York: Cambridge University Press.

Boltanski, L. and Chiapello, E. (2007) *The New Spirit of Capitalism*, London: Verso.

Bonoli, G. (2007) 'Time matters: Postindustrialization, new social risks, and welfare state adaptation in advanced industrial democracies', *Comparative Political Studies*, 40(5), pp 495–520.

Bonoli, G. and Natali, D. (ed) (2012) *The Politics of the New Welfare State*, Oxford: Oxford University Press.

Borghi, V. and van Berkel, R. (2007) 'Individualised service provision in an era of activation and new governance', *International Journal of Sociology and Social Policy*, 27(9–10), pp 413–424.

Bornschier, S. and Kriesi, H. (2015) 'The populist right, the working class, and the changing face of class politics' in J. Rydgren (ed) *Class Politics and the Radical Right*, London: Routledge, pp 10–29.

Bourdieu, P. (1977) *Outline of a Theory of Practice*, Cambridge: Cambridge University Press.

Bourdieu, P. (1987) *Distinction: A Social Critique of the Judgement of Taste*, Cambridge, MA: Harvard University Press.

Bourdieu, P. (2001) *Contre – feux 2 – Pour un mouvement social européen*, Paris: Edition Raison d'Agir.

Bourdieu, P. (2003) 'For a European social movement' in P. Bourdieu (ed) *Firing Back: Against the Tyranny of the Market 2*, London: Verso.

Bourricaud, F. (1981) *The Sociology of Talcott Parsons*, Chicago: University of Chicago Press.

Brady, M. (2007) 'Institutionalised individualism and the care of the self: Single mothers and the state' in C. Howards (ed) *Contested Individualization*, New York: Palgrave Macmillan, pp 187–208.

Brimblecombe, N., Pickard, L., King, D. and Knapp, M. (2017) 'Barriers to receipt of social care services for working carers and the people they care for in times of austerity', *Journal of Social Policy*, 47(2), pp 215–233.

Browe, C. (2017) *Critical Social Theory*, London: Sage.

Brunkhorst, H. (2008) *Habermas*, Florence: Firenze University Press.

Buechl, S.M. (2013) 'Mass society theory' in D.A. Snow, D. Della Porta, B. Klandermans and D. McAdam (eds) *The Wiley-Blackwell Encyclopaedia of Social and Political Movements*, Malden: Blackwell.

Busemeyer, M.R., Rathgeb, P. and Sahm, A.H.J. (2022) 'Authoritarian values and the welfare state: The social policy preferences of radical right voters', *West European Politics*, 45(1), pp 77–101.

Butcher, H., Banks, S. and Henderson, P. (2007) *Critical Community Practice*, Bristol: Policy Press.

Butler, T. and Savage, M. (1995) *Social Change and the Middle Class*, London: UCL Press.

Cantillon, B. (2011) 'The paradox of the social investment state: Growth, employment and poverty in the Lisbon era', *Journal of European Social Policy*, 21(5), pp 432–449.

Cantillon, B. and Vandenbroucke, F. (2014) *Reconciling Work and Poverty Reduction: How Successful are European Welfare States?* Oxford: Oxford University Press.

Case, A. and Deaton, A. (2020) *Deaths of Despair and the Future of Capitalism*, Princeton: Princeton University Press.

Castel, R. (2003) *From Manual Workers to Wage Laborers: Transformation of the Social Question*, New Brunswick: Transaction Publishers.

Castel, R. (2007) *La discrimination négative. Citoyens ou indigènes?*, Paris: Seuil.

Castells, M. (2001) *The Internet Galaxy: Reflections on the Internet, Business and Society*, Oxford: Oxford University Press.

Castells, M. (2012) *Network of Outrage and Hope*, Cambridge: Polity Press.

Chau, R., Foster, L. and Yu, S. (2016) 'Defamilisation and familisation measures: Can they reduce the adverse effects of pro-market pension reforms on women in Hong Kong and the UK?', *Critical Social Policy*, 36(2), pp 205–224.

Clark, C. (2020) *The Dark Knight and the Puppet Master*, London: Penguin Random House.

Clasen, J. and Clegg, D. (2007) 'Levels and levers of conditionality: Measuring change within welfare states' in J. Clasen and N.A. Siegel (eds) *Investigating Welfare State Change: The 'Dependent Variable Problem' in Comparative Analysis*, Cheltenham: Edward Elgar, pp 166–197.

Clayton, R. and Pontusson, J. (1998) 'Welfare-state retrenchment revisited: Entitlement cuts, public sector restructuring, and inegalitarian trends in advanced capitalist societies', *World Politics*, 51(1), pp 67–98.

Cooke, G. and Muir, R. (eds) (2012) *The Relational State: How Recognising the Importance of Human Relationships Could Revolutionise the Role of the State*, London: IPPR.

Corbett, S. and Walker, A. (2017) 'Putting the social back into social policy' in R. Atkinson, L. Mckenzie and S. Winlow (eds) *Building a Better Society*, Bristol: Policy Press, pp 111–124.

Cottam, H. (2011) 'Relational welfare', *Soundings*, 48(11), pp 134–144.

Cramer, K.J. (2016) *The Politics of Resentment: Rural Consciousness in Wisconsin and the Rise of Scott Walker*, Chicago: University of Chicago Press.

Crompton, R. (2008) *Class and Stratification*, Cambridge: Polity Press.

Crouch, C. (2004) *Post-Democracy*, Cambridge: Polity Press.

Crozier, G., Reay, D., James, D., Jamieson, F., Beedell, P., Hollingworth, S. and Williams, K. (2008) 'White middle-class parents, identities, educational choice and the urban comprehensive school: Dilemmas, ambivalence and moral ambiguity', *British Journal of Sociology of Education*, 29(3), pp 261–272.

Cummins, I. (2021) *Welfare and Punishment. From Thatcherism to Austerity*, Bristol: Policy Press.

Dalton, R.J., Flanagan, S.C. and Beck, P.A. (eds) (1984) *Electoral Change in Advanced Industrial Democracies: Realignment or Dealignment?* Princeton: Princeton University Press.

Daly, M.C. (2010) 'Shifts in family policy in the UK under New Labour', *Journal of European Social Policy*, 20(5), pp 433–443.

Dean, H. (2015) *Social Right and Human Welfare*, London: Routledge.

Dean, H. (2020a) *Restoring Social Citizenship in an Age of New Risks*, London: Public Services Trust.

Dean, H. (2020b) *Understanding Human Need*, Bristol: Policy Press.

Deeming, C. and Smyth, P. (2018) *Reframing Global Social Policy*, Bristol: Policy Press.

Della Porta, D. (2015) *Social Movements in Times of Austerity: Ringing Capitalism Back into Protest Analysis*, Cambridge: Polity Press.

Diamond, P. and Liddle, R. (2012) 'Aftershock: The post-crisis social investment welfare state in Europe' in R. Liddle, B. Palier and Palme, J. (eds) *Towards a Social Investment Welfare State? Ideas, Policies and Challenges*, Bristol: Policy Press, pp 285–308.

Donati, P. (2011) *Relational Sociology: A New Paradigm for the Social Sciences*, London: Routledge.

Donati, P. (2021) *Transcending Modernity with Relational Thinking*, London: Routledge.

Donati, P. and Archer, M.S. (2015) *The Relational Subject*, Cambridge: Cambridge University Press.

Dorling, D. (2015) *Injustice: Why Social Inequality Still Persists*, Bristol: Policy Press.

Dorling, D. and Tomlinson, S. (2020) *Rule Britannia: Brexit and the End of Empire*, London: Biteback Publishing.

Duffy, B. (2000) *Satisfaction and expectations: attitudes to public services in deprived areas*, CASE Paper No. 45, London: Centre for Analysis of Social Exclusion, London School of Economics.

Durkheim, E. (1893) *The Division of Labor in Society*, New York: Free Press.

Dwyer, P. (2016) 'Citizenship, conduct and conditionality: Sanction and support in the 21st century UK welfare state', in M. Fenger, J. Hudson and C. Needham (eds) *Social Policy Review 28. Analysis and Debate in Social Policy*, Bristol: Policy Press, pp 41–62.

Dwyer, P. (2017) 'Rewriting the contract? Conditionality, welfare reform and the right and responsibilities of disabled people' in D. Horsfall and J. Hudson (eds) *Social Policy in an Era of Competition*, Bristol: Policy Press, pp 135–148.

Dwyer, P. (2019) *Dealing with Welfare Conditionality: Implementation and Effects*, Bristol: Policy Press.

Eatwell, R. (2005) 'Charisma and the revival of the European extreme right' in J. Rydgren (ed) *Movements of Exclusion: Radical Right-Wing Populism in the Western World*, New York: Nova Science Publishers.

Eatwell, R. and Goodwin, M. (2018) *National Populism: The Revolt Against Liberal Democracy*, London: Pelican.

Elchardus, M. and Spruyt, B. (2016) 'Populism, persistent republicanism and declinism: An empirical analysis of populism as a thin ideology', *Government and Opposition*, 51(1), pp 111–133.

Elias, N. (2001) *The Society of Individuals*, New York: Continuum.

Elliott, A. and Urry, J. (2010) *Mobile Lives*, London: Routledge.

Emmenegger, P., Häusermann, S., Palier, B. and Seeleib-Kaiser, M. (eds) (2012) *The Age of Dualization: The Changing Face of Inequality in Deindustrializing Societies*, Oxford: Oxford University Press.

Enggist, M. and Pingerra, M. (2021) 'Radical right parties and their welfare state stances: Not so blurry after all?', *West European Politics*, 45(1), pp 102–128.

Erikson, R. and Goldthorpe J. (1992) *The Constant Flux*, Oxford: Clarendon Press.

Esping-Andersen, G. (1990) *The Three Worlds of Welfare Capitalism*, Cambridge: Polity Press.

Esping-Andersen, G. (1999) *Social Foundations of Postindustrial Economies*, Oxford: Oxford University Press.

Esping-Andersen, G., Gallie, D., Hemerijck, A. and Myles, J. (2002) *Why We Need a New Welfare State*, Oxford: Oxford University Press.

Etzioni, A. (1995a) *The Spirit of Community*, London: Fontana Press.

Etzioni, A. (ed) (1995b) *New Communitarian Thinking*, Charlottesville: University Press of Virginia.

Etzioni, A. (1996) *The New Golden Rules*, New York: Basic Books.

Eurofound (2015) *Recent Developments in the Distribution of Wages in Europe*, Luxembourg: Publications Office of the European Union.

Eurofound (2018) *Striking a Balance: Reconciling Work and Life in the EU*, Luxembourg: Publications Office of the European Union.

European Commission (2018a) *Informal Care in Europe: Exploring Formalisation, Availability and Quality*, Brussels: European Commission, Directorate-General for Employment, Social Affairs and Inclusion.

European Commission (2018b) *Employment and Social Developments in Europe 2018*, Brussels: Directorate General for Employment, Social Affairs and Inclusion.

European Commission (2018c) *Changes in Child and Family Policies in the EU28 in 2017*, Brussels: European Commission, Directorate-General for Employment, Social Affairs and Inclusion.

European Commission (2019) *Employment and Social Developments in Europe 2019*, Luxembourg: Publications Office of the European Union.

European Commission (2020) *Employment and Social Developments in Europe 2020*, Luxembourg: Publications Office of the European Union.

European Social Survey (ESS) (2018) *The Past, Present and Future of European Welfare Attitudes: Topline Results from Round 8 of the European Social Survey, issue 8*, London: European Research Infrastructure Consortium. Available at: https://www.europeansocialsurvey.org/docs/findings/ESS8_toplines_issue_8_welfare.pdf (accessed 4 May 2022).

Evans, G. and Tilley, J. (2015) 'The new class war: Excluding the working class in 21st-century Britain', *Juncture*, 21(4), pp 298–304.

Evans, G. and Tilley, J. (2017) *The New Politics of Class*, Oxford: Oxford University Press.

Evers, A. (1995) 'Part of the welfare mix: The third sector as an intermediate area', *Voluntas: International Journal of Voluntary and Non-profit Organisations*, 6(2), pp 159–182.

Farnsworth, K. and Irving, Z. (2015) *Social Policy in Times of Austerity*, Bristol: Policy Press.

Fenger, M. (2018) 'The social policy agendas of populist radical right parties in comparative perspective', *Journal of International and Comparative Social Policy*, 34(3), pp 188–209.

Ferrera, M. and Hemerijck, A. (2003) 'Recalibrating Europe's welfare regimes', in J. Zeitlin and D.M. Trubek (eds.), *Governing Work and Welfare in the New Economy: European and American Experiments*, Oxford: Oxford University Press, pp 88–128.

Flint, J. (ed) (2006) *Housing, Urban Governance and Anti-social Behaviour: Perspectives, Policies and Practice*, Bristol: Policy Press.

Florida, R. (2012) *The Rise of the Creative Class Revisited*, tenth anniversary edition, New York: Basic Books.

Flesher Fominaya, C. and Cox, L. (eds) (2013) *Understanding European Movements. New Social Movements, Global Justice Struggles, Anti-Austerity Protest*, London: Routledge.

Fukuyama, F. (2018) *Identity: The Demand for Dignity and the Politics of Resentment*, New York: Farrar, Straus & Giroux.

Funke, M., Schularick, M. and Trebesch, C. (2016) 'Going to extremes: Politics after financial crises, 1870–2014', *European Economic Review*, 88(16), pp 227–260.

Garfinkel, I., Rainwater, L. and Smeeding, T. (2005) *Welfare State Expenditures and the Redistribution of Well-Being, Children, Elderly and Others in Comparative Perspective*, Working Paper 387, Luxembourg: Luxembourg Income Study (LIS).

Gest, J. (2016) *The New Minority: White Working Class Politics in an Age of Immigration and Inequality*, Oxford: Oxford University Press.

Ghysels, J. and Van Launcher W. (2011) 'The unequal benefits of activation: An analysis of the social distribution of family policy among families with young children', *Journal of European Social Policy*, 5(21), pp 472–485.

Giddens, A. (1984) *The Constitution of Society: Outline of the Theory of Structuration*, Cambridge: Polity Press.

Giddens, A. (1991) *Modernity and Self-Identity: Self and Society in the Late Modern Age*, Cambridge: Polity Press.

Giddens, A. (1994) 'Living in a post-traditional society', in U. Beck, A. Giddens, and S. Lash (eds), *Reflexive Modernisation: Politics, Tradition and Aesthetics in the Modern Social Order*, Cambridge: Polity Press, pp 56–109.

Giddens, A. (1998) *The Third Way: The Renewal of Social Democracy*, Cambridge: Polity Press.

Giddens, A. (2006) *Sociology*, Cambridge: Polity Press.

Giddens, A. (2007) *Europe in a Global Age*, Cambridge: Polity Press.

Gidron, N. and Hall, P. (2017) 'The politics of social status: Economic and cultural roots of the populist right', *The British Journal of Sociology*, 68(suppl. 1), pp 57–84.

Gidron, N. and Hall, P.A. (2019) 'Populism as a problem of social integration', *Comparative Political Studies*, 53(7), pp 1027–1059.

Gilchrist, A. (2009) *The Well-Connected Community: A Networking Approach to Community Development*, Bristol: Policy Press.

Gilchrist, A. and Taylor, M. (2022) *The Short Guide to Community Development*, Bristol: Policy Press.

Gingrich, J. and Häusermann, S. (2015) 'The decline of the working-class vote, the reconfiguration of the welfare support coalition and consequences for the welfare state', *Journal of European Social Policy*, 25(1), pp 50–75.

Giugni, M. and Grasso, M.T. (2019) *Street Citizens: Protest Politics and Social Movement Activism in the Age of Globalization*, Cambridge: Cambridge University Press.

Givens, T. (2005) *Voting Radical Right in Western Europe*, New York: Cambridge University Press.

Golder, M. (2016) 'Far-right parties in Europe', *Annual Review of Political Science*, 19(1), pp 477–497.

Goldthorpe, J.H. (1987) *Social Mobility and Class Structure in Modern Britain*, Oxford: Clarendon Press.

Goldthorpe, J.H. and McKnight, A. (2004) *The Economic Basis of Social Class*, CASE Paper 80, London School of Economics.

Goodin, R.E. and Le Grand, J. (1987) *Not Only the Poor: The Middle Classes and the Welfare State*, London: Allen & Unwin.

Grasso, M. and Giugni, M. (eds) (2022) *The Routledge Handbook of Environmental Movements*, London: Routledge.

Greve, B. (2019) *Welfare, Populism and Welfare Chauvinism*, Bristol: Policy Press.

Greve, B. (2020) *Austerity, Retrenchment and the Welfare State: Truth or Fiction?*, Cheltenham: Edward Elgar.

Griggs, J. and Evans, M. (2010) *Sanctions Within Conditional Benefit Systems: A Review of Evidence*, York: Joseph Rowntree Foundation.

Grusky, D. B. and Weisshaar, K. (ed) (2014) *Social Stratification, Class, Race and Gender in Sociological Perspective*, New York: Routledge.

Gugushvili, D. and Laenen, T. (2019) *Twenty Years after Korpi and Palme's 'Paradox of Redistribution': What Have We Learned so Far, and Where Should We Take it From Here?*, SPSW Working Paper No. 5, Leuven: Centre for Sociological Research, KU Leuven.

Guilluy, C. (2018) 'France is deeply fractured: Gilets jaunes are just a symptom', *The Guardian*, 2 December. www.theguardian.com/commentisfree/2018/dec/02/france-is-deeply-fractured-gilets-jeunes-just-a-symptom (accessed 5 February 2022).

Habermas, J. (1984) *The Theory of Communicative Action: Reason and the Razionalization of Society*, Vol 1. Boston: Beacon Press.

Habermas, J. (1987) *The Theory of Communicative Action: Lifeworld and System*, Vol 2. Boston: Beacon Press.

Habermas, J. (1992) 'Further reflections on the public sphere' in C. Calhoun (ed) *Habermas and the Public Sphere*, Cambridge, MA: MIT Press, pp 421–461.

Habermas, J. (1996) *Between Facts and Norms: Contributions to a Discourse Theory of Law and Democracy*, Cambridge, MA: MIT Press.

Hacker, J.S. (2002) *The Divided Welfare State: The Battle over Public and Private Social Benefits in the United States*, Cambridge: Cambridge University Press.

Hacker, J.S. (2004) 'Privatising risk without privatising the welfare state, the hidden politics of social policy retrenchment in the United States', *American Political Science Review*, 98(2), pp 243–260.

Hacker, J.S. (2010) *The Great Risk Shift: The New Economic Insecurity and the Decline of the American Dream*, New York: Oxford University Press:.

Hacker, J.S. (2013) 'How US politics is undermining the American Dream, and what it means for the UK' in S. Parker (ed) *The Squeezed Middle: The Pressure on Ordinary Workers in America and Britain*, Bristol: Policy Press, pp 143–153.

Hacker, J.S. and Pierson, P. (2010) *Winner-Take-All Politics: How Washington made the Rich Richer – and Turned its Back on the Middle Class*, New York: Simon & Schuster.

Hacker, J.S. and Pierson, P. (2020) *Let Them Eat Tweets*, New York: Liveright Publishing Corporation.

Hainsworth, P. (ed) (2000) *The Politics of the Extreme Right: From the Margins to the Mainstream*, London: Pinter.

Hall, P. (1993) 'Policy paradigms, social learning, and the state: The case of economic policymaking in Britain', *Comparative Politics*, 25(2), pp 275–296.

Hamilton, R. (2001) *Mass Society, Pluralism, and Bureaucracy: Explication, Assessment and Commentary*, Westport, CT: Praeger Publisher.

Hänninen, S., Lehtelä, K.M. and Saikkonen, P. (eds) (2019) *The Relational Nordic Welfare State: Between Utopia and Ideology*, Cheltenham: Edward Elgar.

Hansen, M.P. (2019) *The Moral Economy of Activation: Ideas, Politics and Policies*, Bristol: Policy Press.

Harrison, M. and Reeve, K. (2002) 'Social welfare movements and collective action: Lessons from two UK housing cases', *Housing Studies*, 17(5), pp 755–771.

Harrison, M. and Sanders, T. (eds) (2014) *Social Policies and Social Control: New Perspective on the 'Not-so-Big Society'*, Bristol: Policy Press.

Harvey, D. (2007) 'Neoliberalism as creative destruction', *The Annals of the American Academy of Political and Social Science*, 610(1), pp 22–44.

Harvey, D. (2016) *The Ways of the World*, Oxford: Oxford University Press.

Hastings, A. (2009) 'Poor neighbourhoods and poor services: Evidence on the "rationing" of environmental service provision to deprived neighborhoods', *Urban Studies*, 46(13), pp 2907–2927.

Häusermann, S. (2012) 'The politics of old and new social policies' in G. Bonoli and D. Natali (eds) *The Politics of the New Welfare State*, Oxford: Oxford University Press, pp 111–132.

Häusermann, S. and Palier, B. (2017) 'The politics of social investment: Policy legacies and class coalitions' in A. Hemerijck (ed) *The Uses of Social Investment*, Oxford: Oxford University Press, pp 339–348.

Heimburg, D.V. and Ness, O. (2021) 'Relational welfare: A socially just response to co-creating health and wellbeing for all', *Scandinavian Journal of Public Health*, 49(6), pp 639–652.

Henderson, P. and Thomas, D.N. (2013) *Skills in Neighbourhood Work*, London: Routledge.

Hertz, N. (2020) *The Lonely Century: Coming Together in a World that's Pulling Apart*, London: Hodder & Stoughton.

Hill, M. and Irving, Z. (2020) *Exploring the World of Social Policy*, Bristol: Policy Press.

Hodge, R.W. and Treiman, D.J. (1968) 'Class identification in the United States', *American Journal of Sociology*, 73(5), pp 535–547.

Horner, R., Schindler, S., Haberly, D. and Aoyama, Y. (2018) 'Globalisation, uneven development and the North-South "big switch"', *Cambridge Journal of Regions, Economy and Society*, 11(1), pp 17–33.

Horsfall D. and Hudson, J. (ed) (2017) *Social Policy in an Era of Competition*, Bristol: Policy Press.

Hout, M. (2008) 'How class works: Objective and subjective aspects of class since the 1970s' in A. Lareau and D. Conley (eds) *Social Class: How Does Work?* New York: Russell Sage Foundation, pp 25–64.

Howard, C. (2007) 'Three models of individualised biography' in C. Howard (ed) *Contested Individualization: Debates about Contemporary Personhood*, Hampshire: Palgrave Macmillan, pp 25–43.

Humpage, L. (2015) *Policy Change, Public Attitudes and Social Citizenship*, Bristol: Policy Press.

Ignazi, P. (2003) *Extreme Right Parties in Western Europe*, Oxford: Oxford University Press.

Immervoll, H. and Knotz, C. (2018) *How Demanding Are Activation Requirements for Jobseekers?*, Bonn: IZA Institute for Labour Economics.

Ivarsflaten, E. (2005) 'The vulnerable populist right parties: No economic realignment fuelling their electoral success', *European Journal of Political Research*, 44(3), pp 465–492.

Jacobsen, H.V. and Marshman, S. (2008) 'Bauman's etaphors: The poetic imagination in sociology', *Current Sociology*, 56(5), pp 798–818.

Jetten, J., Mols, F. and Selvanathan, H.P. (2020) 'How economic inequality fuels the rise and persistence of the yellow vest movement', *International Review of Social Psychology*, 33(1), pp 1–12.

Juul, S. (2013) *Solidarity in Individualised Societies: Recognition, Justice and Good Judgement*, New York: Routledge.

Kallenberg, A.L. (2018) *Precarius Lives: Job Insecurity and Well-Being in Rich Democracies*, Cambridge: Polity Press.

Kitschel, H. and McGann, A. J. (1997) *The Radical Right in Western Europe: A Comparative Analysis*, Ann Arbor: University of Michigan Press.

Kitschelt, H. and Hellemans, S. (1990) *Beyond the European Left*, Durham, NC: Duke University Press.

Klandermans, B. and Mayer, N. (eds) (2006) *Extreme Right Activists in Europe*, London: Routledge.

Koopmans, R., Statham, P., Giugni, M. and Passy, F. (2005) *Contested Citizenship: Immigration and Cultural Diversity in Europe*, Minneapolis: University of Minneapolis Press.

Kornhauser, W. (2017 [1959]) *The Politics of Mass Society (with a new introduction by Irving Louis Horowitz)*, New York: Routledge.

Kriesi, H. (1998) 'The transformation of cleavage politics: The 1997 Stein Rokkan lecture', *European Journal of Political Research*, 33(2), pp 165–185.

Krugman P. (2009) *The Conscience of a Liberal*, New York: Norton & Company.

Kus, B. (2013) 'Credit, consumption, and debt: Comparative perspectives', *International Journal of Comparative Sociology*, 54(3), pp 183–186.

Lambie-Mumford, H. (2019) 'The growth of food banks in Britain and what they mean for social policy', *Critical Social Policy*, 39(1), pp 3–22.

Lambie-Mumford, H. and Silvasti, T. (eds) (2021) *The Rise of Food Charity in Europe*, Bristol: Policy Press.

Langenbucher, K. (2015) *How Demanding are Eligibility Criteria for Unemployment Benefits? Quantitative Indicators for OECD and EU Countries*, Social, Employment and Migration Working Paper, 166, Paris: OECD Publishing.

Lapidus, J. (2019) *The Quest for a Divided Welfare State*, Basingstoke: Palgrave Macmillan.

Larsen, J.E. (2005) 'The active society and activation policy: Ideologies, contexts and effects' in J.G. Andersen, A.M. Guillemard, P.H. Jensen and B. Pfau-Effinger (eds) *The Changing Face of Welfare: Consequences and Outcomes from a Citizenship Perspective*, Bristol: Policy Press, pp 135–150.

Lash, S. (1994) 'Reflexivity and its doubles: Structure, aesthetics, community' in U. Beck, A. Giddens and S. Lash (eds) *Reflexive Modernisation: Politics, Tradition and Aesthetics in the Modern Social Order*, Cambridge: Polity Press, pp 110–173.

Lash, S. (1999) *Another Modernity: A Different Rationality*, Oxford: Blackwell.

Lawler, S. and Payne, G. (2018) *Social Mobility for the 21st Century*, London: Routledge.

Le Grand, J. (1982) *The Strategy of Equality, Redistribution and the Social Services*, London: Allen & Unwin.

Le Grand, J. and Winter, D. (1986) 'The middle-classes and the welfare state under Conservative and Labour governments', *Journal of Public Policy*, 6(4), pp 399–430.

Levy, J.D. (1999) 'Vice into virtue? Progressive politics and welfare reform in continental Europe', *Politics and Society*, 27(2), pp 239–273.

Levy, J.D. (2012) 'Welfare retrenchment' in F. Castles, S. Leibfried, J. Lewis, H. Obinger and C. Pierson (eds) *The Oxford Handbook of the Welfare State*, Oxford: Oxford University Press, pp 552–565.

Lind, M. (2004) 'We are still a middle-class nation?', *The Atlantic Monthly*, 293(1), pp 120–128.

Lipset, S.M. (1959) 'Social stratification and right-wing extremism', *British Journal of Sociology*, 10(4), pp 346–382.

Lipset, S.M. (1960) *Political Man: The Social Bases of Politics*, Garden City: Doubleday.

Lipset, S.M. (1994) 'The social requisites of democracy revisited: 1993 presidential address', *American Sociological Review*, 59(1), pp 1–22.

Lipset, S.M. and Rokkan, S. (1967) 'Cleavage structures, party systems, and voter alignments: An introduction' in S.M. Lipset and S. Rokkan (eds) *Party Systems and Voter Alignments: Crossnational Perspectives*, New York: Free Press, pp 1–67.

Lister, R. (1994) ' "She has other duties": Women, citizenship and social security' in S Baldwin and J. Falkingham (eds) *Social Security and Social Change: New Challenges to the Beveridge Model*, Hempel Hempstead: Harvester Wheatsheaf, pp 31–44.

Lister, R. (2011) 'The age of responsibility: Social policy and citizenship in the early 21st century' in C. Holden, M. Kilkey and G. Ramia (eds) *Social Policy Review 23*, Bristol: Policy Press/Social Policy Association, pp 63–84.

Lockwood, D. (1964) 'Social integration and system integration' in G.K. Zollschan and W. Hirsch (eds) *Explorations in Social Change*, Boston: Houghton Mifflin Company, pp 249–267.

Mahon, R. (2013) 'Social investment according to the OECD/DELSA: A discourse in the making', *Global Policy*, 4(2), pp 150–159.

Marcuse, H. (1964) *One-Dimensional Man: Studies in the Ideology of Advanced Industrial Society*, Boston: Beacon Press.

Martin, G. (2015) *Understanding Social Movements*, London: Routledge.

Martin, J.P. (2015) 'Activation and active labour market policies in OECD countries: Stylised facts and evidence on their effectiveness', *IZA Journal of Labor Policy*, 4(4), pp 1–29.

Mathijs, K. and Coenders, M. (2019) 'Explaining differences in welfare chauvinism between and within individuals over time: The role of subjective and objective economic risk, economic egalitarianism, and ethnic threat', *European Sociological Review*, 35(6), pp 860–873.

Matthews, P. and Hastings, A. (2013) 'Middle-class political activism and middle-class advantage in relation to public services: A realist synthesis of the evidence base', *Social Policy and Administration*, 47(1), pp 72–92.

Mätzke, M. and Ostner, I. (2010) 'Introduction: Change and continuity in recent family policies', *Journal of European Social Policy*, 20(5), pp 387–398.

Mau, S. (2015) *Inequality, Marketisation and the Majority Class: Why Did the European Middle-Classes Accept Neo-Liberalism*, New York: Palgrave Macmillan.

Mayhew, D. (2000) 'Electoral realignments', *Annual Review of Political Science*, 3(1), pp 449–474.

McCann, P. (2016) *The UK Regional–national Economic Problem: Geography, Globalisation and Governance*, London: Routledge.

Mendoza, X. and Vernis, A. (2008) 'The changing role of governments and the emergence of the relational state', *Corporate Governance*, 8(4), pp 389–396.

Merton, R.K. (1968) 'The Matthew effect in science', *Science*, 159(3810), pp 56–63.

Milkman, R. (2017) 'A new political generation: Millennials and the post-2008 wave of protest', *American Sociological Review*, 1(82), pp 1–31.

Mills, C.W. (1951) *White Collar*, New York: Oxford University Press.

Minkenberg, M. (2000) 'The renewal of the radical right: Between modernity and anti-modernity', *Government and Opposition*, 35(2), pp 170–188.

Minkenberg, M. (2016) 'The West European radical right as a collective actor: Modeling the impact of cultural and structural variables on party formation and movement mobilization', *Comparative European Politics*, 1(29), pp 149–170.

Morel, N., Palier, B. and Palme, J. (eds) (2012) *Towards a Social Investment Welfare State? Ideas, Policies, Challenges*, Bristol: Policy Press.

Morel, N., Palier, B. and Palme, J. (2013) *The Social Investment Welfare State in Europe, 1990s and 2000s: Economic Ideas and Social Policies*, Working Paper Series No. 33, Paris: Sciences Po.

Mudde, C. (2007) *Populist Radical Right Parties in Europe*, Cambridge: Cambridge University Press.

Mulgan, G. (2012) 'Government with the people: The outlines of a relational state', in G. Cook and R. Muir (eds) *The Relational State: How Recognising the Importance of Human Relationships Could Revolutionise the Role of the State*, London: IPPR, pp 20–34.

Murray, C. (2013) *Coming Apart: The State of White America, 1960–2010*, New York: Random House.

Murray, R. (2009) *Danger and Opportunity: Crisis and the New Social Economy*, London: NESTA.

Muzergues, T. (2020) *The Great Class Shift: How New Social Class Structures are Redefining Western Politics*, London: Routledge.

Needham, C. (2011) *Personalising Public Services: Understanding the Personalisation Narrative*, Bristol: Policy Press.

Norris, P. (2005) *Radical Right, Parties and Electoral Competition*, Cambridge: Cambridge University Press.

Norris, P. and Inglehart, R. (2019) *Cultural Backlash: Trump, Brexit, and Authoritarian Populism*, Cambridge: Cambridge University Press.

Oberschall, A. (1973) *Social Conflict and Social Movements*, Englewood Cliffs: Prentice-Hall.

OECD (2016) *The Squeezed Middle Class in OECD and Emerging Countries: Myth and Reality*, Paris: OECD.

OECD (2019) *Under Pressure: The Squeezed Middle Class*, Paris: OECD.

Oesch, D. (2008) 'Explaining workers' support for right-wing populist parties in western Europe: Evidence from Austria, Belgium, France, Norway, and Switzerland', *International Political Science Review*, 29(3), pp 349–373.

Palier, B. (ed) (2010) *A Long Goodbye to Bismarck: The Politics of Welfare Reform in Continental Europe*, Amsterdam: Amsterdam University Press.

Palier, B. (2012) 'Turning vice into vice: How Bismarckian welfare states have gone from unsustainability to dualization' in G. Bonoli, and B. Natali (eds) *The Politics of the New Welfare State*, Oxford: Oxford University Press.

Palier, B. and Kathleen, T. (2010) 'Institutionalizing dualism: Complementarities and change in France and Germany', *Politics and Society*, 38(1), pp 119–148.

Papadopoulos, T. and Roumpakis, A. (2019) 'Family as a socio-economic actor in the political economy of welfare' in E. Heins, J. Rees and C. Needham (eds) *Social Policy Review*, 31, Bristol: Policy Press, pp 243–266.

Parker, S. (ed) (2013) *The Squeezed Middle: The Pressure on Ordinary Workers in America and Britain*, Bristol: Policy Press.

Parsell, C., Clarke, A. and Perales, F. (2022) *Charity and Poverty in Advanced Welfare States*, London: Routledge.

Parsons, T. (1937) *The Structure of Social Action*, New York: McGraw-Hill.

Parsons, T. (1962) 'Youth in the context of American society', *Daedalus* 91(1), pp 97–123.

Parsons, T. (1978) *Action, Theory and the Human Condition*, New York: Free Press.

Pawson, R. (2006) *Evidence-based Policy: A Realist Perspective*, London: Sage.

Pawson, R. and Tilley, N. (1997) *Realistic Evaluation*, London: Sage.

Payne, G. (ed) (2013) *Social Divisions*, Basingstoke: Palgrave Macmillan.

Payne, G. (2018) 'Social mobility: which ways now' in S. Lawler and G. Payne (eds) *Social Mobility for the 21st Century*, London: Routledge, pp 13–24.

Pierson, C. (1991) *Beyond the Welfare State*, 2nd edition, Cambridge: Polity Press.

Pierson, C. (2021) *The Next Welfare State*, Bristol: Policy Press.

Pierson, P. (1994) *Dismantling the Welfare State? Reagan, Thatcher and the Politics of Retrenchmen t*, Cambridge: Cambridge University Press.

Piketty, T. (2014) *Capital in the Twenty-First Century*, Cambridge, MA: Harvard University Press.

Pintelon, O., Cantillon, B. and Van den Bosch, K. (2013) 'The social stratification of social risks: The relevance of class for social investment strategies', *Journal of European Social Policy*, 23(1), pp 52–67.

Pitchford, M. (2008) *Making Spaces for Community Development*, Bristol: Policy Press.

Porpora, D.V. (2015) 'Why don't things change? The matter of morphostasis' in M. Archer (ed) *Generative Mechanisms Transforming the Social Order, Social Morphogenesis*, Cham: Springer, pp 185–203.

Powell, M. (1995) 'The strategy of equality revisited', *Journal of Social Policy*, 24(2), pp 163–185.

Pressman, S. (2007) 'The decline of the middle class: An international perspective', *Journal of Economic Issues*, 41(1), pp 181–200.

Pressman, S. (2017) 'Why has the Italian middle class remained so constant', *Sociologia e Politiche Sociali*, 20(2), pp 45–66.

Rathgeb, P. and Busemeyer, M.R. (2022) 'How to study the populist radical right and the welfare state?', *West European Politics*, 45(1), pp 1–23.

Rattansi, A. (2017) *Bauman and Contemporary Sociology: A Critical Analysis*, Manchester: Manchester University Press.

Ravallion, M. (2010) 'The developing world's bulging but vulnerable middle class', *World Development*, 38(4), pp 445–454.

Rigney, D. (2010) *The Matthew Effect: How Advantage Begets Further Advantage*, New York: Columbia University Press.

Rodríguez-Pose, A. (2018) 'The revenge of the places that don't matter (and what to do about it)', *Cambridge Journal of Regions, Economy and Society*, 11(1), pp 189–209.

Rosa, H. (2015) *Social Acceleration: A New Theory of Modernity*, New York: Columbia University Press.

Rose, D. and Harrison, E. (2007) 'The European socio-economic classification: A new social class schema for comparative European research', *European Societies*, 9(3), 459–490.

Rose, N. (1996) 'The death of the social? Re-figuring the territory of government', *Economy and Society*, 25(3), 327–356.

Rose, N. (1999) *Powers of Freedom: Reframing Political Thought*, Cambridge: Cambridge University Press.

Rose, N. (2008) 'The death of the social' in P. Miller and N. Rose, *Governing the Present*, Cambridge: Polity Press, pp 54–84.

Rothstein, B. (1998) *Just Institutions Matter: The Moral and Political Logic of the Universal Welfare State*, New York: Cambridge University Press.

Rothstein, B. and Stolle, D. (2008) 'The state and social capital: An institutional theory of generalized trust', *Comparative Politics*, 40(4), pp 441–459.

Rubery, J. (2007) 'Developing segmentation theory, a third year perspective', *Economies et Sociétés*, 28(6), pp 911–964.

Rueda, D. (2005) 'Insider–outsider politics in industrialised democracies: The challenge to social democratic parties', *American Political Science Review*, 99(1), pp 61–74.

Russel Hochschild, A. (2003) *The Commercialization of Intimate Life*, Los Angeles: University of California Press.

Rydgren, J. (2007) 'The sociology of the radical right', *Annual Review of Sociology*, 33(1), pp 241–262.

Rydgren, J. (ed) (2015) *Class Politics and the Radical Right*, London: Routledge.

Saraceno, C. and Keck, W. (2010) 'Can we indentify intergenerational policy regimes in Europe?', *European Societies*, 12(5), pp 675–696.

Sassen, S. (2014) *Expulsions Brutality and Complexity in the Global Economy*, Cambridge, MA: Harvard University Press.

Savage, M. (2015) *Social Class in the 21st Century*, London: Pelican Books.

Savage, M. and Butler, T. (1995) 'Assets and the middle class in contemporary Britain' in T. Butler and M. Savage, *Social Change and the Middle Class*, London: UCL Press, pp 345–357.

Savage, M., Devine, F., Cunningham, N., Taylor, M., Li, Y., Hjellbrekke, J., et al (2015) 'A new model of social class? Findings from the BBC's Great British Class Survey experiment', *Sociology*, 2(47), pp 219–250.

Saxonberg, S. (2013) 'From defamilisation to degenderization: Toward a new welfare typology', *Social Policy and Administration*, 47(1), pp 26–49.

Schmidtke, O. (ed) (2002) 'Transforming the social democratic left: The challenges to third way politics in the age of globalisation' in O. Schmidtke, *The Third Way Transformation of Social Democracy: Normative Claims and Policy Initiatives in the 21st Century*, New York: Routledge, pp 3–27.

Schreurs, S. (2021) 'Those were the days: Welfare nostalgia and the populist radical right in the Netherlands, Austria and Sweden', *Journal of International and Comparative Social Policy*, 37(2), pp 128–141.

Schumacher, G. and van Kersbergen, K. (2016) 'Do mainstream parties adapt to the welfare chauvinism of populist parties?', *Party Politics*, 22(3), pp 300–312.

Sciortino, G. (2016) 'American society and the societal community: Talcott Parsons, citizenship and diversity', in J. Treviño (ed) *The Anthem Companion to Talcott Parsons*, New York: Anthem Press, pp 191–206.

Scott, J. (2013) 'Three core social divisions' in G. Payne (ed) *Social Divisions*, Basingstoke: Palgrave Macmillan, pp 25–67.

Seeleib-Kaiser, M., Saunders, A. and Naczyk, M. (2011) 'Shifting the public-private mix: A new dualization of welfare?' in P. Emmenegger, S. Häusermann, B. Palier and M. Seeleib-Kaiser (eds) *The Age of Dualization: The Changing Face of Inequality in Deindustrializing Societies*, Oxford: Oxford University Press, pp 151–175.

Sennett, R. (1998) *The Corrosion of Character: The Personal Consequences of Work in the New Capitalism*, New York: W.W. Norton and Co.

Sennett, R. (2006) *The Culture of the New Capitalism*, New Haven: Yale University Press.

Shafik, M. (2021) *What We Owe Each Other: A New Social Contract*, Princeton: Princeton University Press.

Siegmann, A. (ed) (2019) *The Middle: The Middle Class as the Moral Core of Society*, Brussels: Wilfried Martens Centre for European Studies.

Simmel G. (1971) 'How is society possible?' in G. Simmel (ed) *On Individuality and Social Forms*, with an Introduction by D.N. Levine, Chicago: The University of Chicago Press, pp 6–22.

Siza, R. (2017) 'Welfare for the middle class: The case of reinforcement', *Sociologia e Politiche Sociali*, 20(2), pp 25–44.

Siza, R. (2019) 'Declines and divisions: The missing welfare needs of the majority', *Journal of International and Comparative Social Policy*, 2(35), pp 211–226.

Siza, R. (2022) 'In the midst of the COVID-19 pandemic: Economic insecurity and coping strategies of Italian households', *International Journal of Sociology and Social Policy*, 42(3–4), pp 298–312.

Smeeding, T.M. (2005) 'Public policy, economic inequality and poverty: The United States in comparative perspective', *Social Science Quarterly*, 86(1), pp 955–983.

Somers, M.R. (2008) *Genealogies of Citizenship: Markets, Statelessness, and the Rights to Have Rights*, New York: Cambridge University Press.

Sørensen M.P. and Christiansen, A. (2013) *Ulrich Beck. An Introduction to the Theory of Second Modernity and the Risk Society*, London: Routledge.

Spicker, P. (2019) *Thinking Collectively: Social Policy, Collective Action and the Common Good*, Bristol: Policy Press.

Standing, G. (2011) *The Precariat: The New Dangerous Class*, London: Bloomsbury Academic.

Standing, G. (2014) *A Precariat Charter: From Denizens to Citizens*, London: Bloomsbury Academic.

Starke, P. (2008) *Radical Welfare State Retrenchment: A Comparative Analysis*, Basingstoke: Palgrave.

Steinmetz, G. (1998) 'Critical realism and historical sociology: A review article', *Comparative Studies in Society and History*, 40(1), pp 170–186.

Stiglitz, J. (2015) *The Great Divide: Unequal Societies and What We Can Do About Them*, New York: Norton.

Stiglitz J. E. (2016) *Rewriting the rules of the American economy*, New York: W. W. Norton & Company.

Streeck, W. (2016) *How Will Capitalism End?*, London: Verso.

Svallfors, S. (ed) (2007) *The Political Sociology of the Welfare State: Institutions, Social Cleavages, and Orientations*, Stanford, CA: Stanford University Press.

Swank, D. and Betz, H.G. (2019) 'Do radical right populist parties matter? The case of the European welfare state' in *American Political Science Association. Annual Meeting and Exhibition*, Washington, DC, 29 August 2019–1 September 2019, pp 1–49.

Tavory, I. and Goodman, Y. (2009) ' "A collective of individuals": Between self and solidarity in a rainbow gathering', *Sociology of Religion*, 70(3), pp 262–284.

Taylor-Gooby, P. (1985) *Public Opinion, Ideology and State Welfare*, London: Routledge.

Taylor-Gooby, P. (2013) *The Double Crisis of the Welfare State and What We Can Do About It*, Basingstoke: Palgrave Macmillan.

Taylor-Gooby, P. (2016) 'The divisive welfare state', *Social Policy and Administration*, 50(6), pp 712–733.

Taylor-Gooby, P. and Leruth, B. (eds) (2018) *Attitudes, Aspirations and Welfare: Social Policy Directions in Uncertain Times*, Basingstoke: Palgrave Macmillan.

Taylor-Gooby, P., Gumy, J.M. and Otto, A. (2015) 'Can "new welfare" address poverty through more and better jobs?', *Journal of Social Policy*, 44(1), pp 83–104.

Taylor-Gooby, P., Leruth, B. and Chung, H. (2017) *After Austerity: Welfare State Transformation in Europe after Great Recession*, Oxford: Oxford University Press.

Thurow, L. (1984) 'The disappearance of middle class', *New York Times*, February 5.

Titmuss, R.M. (1958) *Essays on the Welfare State*, London: Allen & Unwin.

Törnqvist, M. (2019) 'Living alone together: Individualised collectivism in Swedish communal housing', *Sociology*, 53(5), pp 900–915.

Touraine, A. (1969) *La société post-industrielle*, Paris: Denoël.

Touraine, A. (1974) *Pour la Sociologie*, Paris: Editions du Seuil.

Touraine, A. (1992) *Critique de la Modernite*, Paris: Fayard.

Touraine, A. (2014) *After the Crisis*, Cambridge: Polity Press.

Trenz, H.J. and Grasso, M. (2018) 'Toward a new conditionality of welfare? Reconsidering solidarity in the Danish welfare state' in C. Lahusen and M.T. Grasso (eds) *Solidarity in Europe: Citizens' Responses in Times of Crisis*, Basingstoke: Palgrave Macmillan, pp 19–42.

Turner, R. and Killian, L. (1987) *Collective Behaviour*, Englewood Cliffs: Prentice-Hall.

Tussing, A.D. (1974) 'The dual welfare system', *Society*, 11(2), pp 50–57.

Vaalavuo, M. (2013) 'The redistributive impact of "old" and "new" social spending', *Journal of Social Policy*, 3(42), pp 513–539.

Valkenburg, B. (2007) 'Individualising activation services: Thrashing out an ambiguous concept' in R. Van Berkel and B. Valkenburg (eds) *Making it Personal: Individualising Activation Services in the EU*, Bristol: Policy Press.

Van Aelst, P. and Walgrave, S. (2001) 'Who is that (wo)man in the street? From the normalisation of protest to the normalisation of the protester', *European Journal of Political Research*, 39(4), pp 461–486.

Van Kersbergen, K. and Hemerijck, A. (2012) 'Two decades of change in Europe: The emergence of the social investment state', *Journal of Social Policy*, 41(3), pp 475–492.

Van Loon, J. (2002) *Risk and Technological Culture: Towards a Sociology of Virulence*, London: Routledge.

van Oorschot, W. (2000) 'Who should get what, and why? On deservingness criteria and the conditionality of solidarity among the public', *Policy & Politics*, 28(1), pp 33–48.

van Oorschot, W. (2006) 'Making the difference in social Europe: Deservingness perceptions among citizens of European welfare states', *Journal of European Social Policy*, 16(1), pp 23–42.

van Vliet, O. and Wang, C. (2015) 'Social investment and poverty reduction: A comparative analysis across fifteen European countries', *Journal of Social Policy*, 44(3), pp 611–638.

Verschraegen, G. (2011) 'Istitutionalised individualism: Parsons and Luhmann on American society' in H. Bergthaller and C. Schinko (eds) *Addressing Modernity: Social Systems Theory and US Cultures*, Amsterdam: Rodopi, pp 171–200.

Watts, B. and Fitzpatrick, S. (2018) *Welfare Conditionality*, London: Routledge.

Watts, B., Fitzpatrick, S., Bramley, G. and Watkins, D. (2014) *Welfare Sanctions and Conditionality in the UK*, York: Joseph Rowntree Foundation.

Weber, M. (1968) *Economy and Society: An Outline of Interpretative Sociology*, Vol 1, New York: Bedminster Press.

Whelan, C. T., Nolan, B. and Maitre, B. (2017) 'Polarization or squeezed middle in the great recession?: A comparative European analysis of the distribution of economic stress', *Social Indicators Research*, 133(1), 163–184.

Wilensky, H.L. (1961) 'Orderly careers and social participation: The impact of work history on social integration in the middle mass', *American Sociological Review*, 26(4), pp 521–539.

Wilensky, H.L. (1975) *The Welfare State and Equality: Structural and Ideological Roots of Public Expenditure*, Berkeley: University of California Press.

Wilensky, H.L. (1976) *The 'New Corporatism', Centralisation, and the Welfare State*, London: SAGE.

Wilensky, H.L. (2002) *Rich Democracies: Political Economy, Public Policy, and Performance*, Berkeley: University of California Press.

Williams, F. (2021) *Social Policy: A Critical and Intersectional Analysis*, Cambridge: Polity Press.

Wilson, W.J. (1987) *The Truly Disadvantaged: The Inner City, the Underclass, and Public Policy*, Chicago: University of Chicago Press.

Zagel, H. and Lohmann, H. (2020) 'Conceptual approaches in comparative family policy research' in R. Nieuwenhuis and W. Van Lancker (eds) *The Palgrave Handbook of Family Policy*, Basingstoke: Palgrave Macmillan, pp 119–140.

Index